EARLY YEARS
ACTIVITY CHEST

Multicultural activities

British Library Cataloguing-in-Publication Data
A catalogue record for this book is available from the British Library.

ISBN 0 439 01728 9

ACKNOWLEDGEMENTS

The publishers gratefully acknowledge permission to reproduce the following copyright material:

Barbara Moore for 'Holi'; 'Divali'; 'The story of the banyan tree'; 'The story of Chinese New Year'; 'The story of Hanukkah'; 'The story of the Dragon Boat Race'; 'The story of the mehndi tree' © 2000, Barbara Moore. All previously unpublished.

Every effort has been made to trace copyright holders and the publishers apologize for any inadvertent omissions.

AUTHOR
Carole Court

EDITOR
Sally Gray

ASSISTANT EDITOR
Lesley Sudlow

SERIES DESIGNER
Lynne Joesbury

DESIGNER
Lynne Joesbury

ILLUSTRATIONS
Debbie Clark

COVER PHOTOGRAPH
Fiona Pragoff

Text © 2000 Carole Court
© 2000 Scholastic Ltd

Designed using Adobe Pagemaker
Published by Scholastic Ltd, Villiers House,
Clarendon Avenue, Leamington Spa, Warwickshire CV32 5PR

Visit our website at www.scholastic.co.uk

3 4 5 6 7 8 9   2 3 4 5 6 7 8 9 0

CONTENTS

CONTENTS

Introduction

The aims of the series

This book forms part of a series that provides activities useful for filling pockets of time in a productive and enjoyable way. You will find a mixture of activities suitable for younger children which help them to practise skills and enjoy experiences across all the areas of the early years curriculum.

How to use this book

The six activity chapters each relate to one of the six areas of the Early Learning Goals and contain eight activities each. There are activities to encourage early personal, social and emotional development, communication, language and literacy skills, mathematical development, knowledge and understanding of the world, physical development and creative development. The activities are timed and can be dipped into and used in a productive and useful way.

Each activity is described using the same headings for ease of use, with full details of what you will need, any preparation required, step-by-step instructions and advice on carrying out the activity. Differentiation is provided for younger and older children and ways of maintaining links with home and follow-up ideas are also given.

How to use the photocopiable pages

The 24 photocopiable pages are a mixture of stories, rhymes, activities and display material. They have been designed to be used in a flexible way. For example, as well as reading the stories to the children you may like to enlarge copies of them and display them for parents and carers to read, or you may choose to send home copies of the stories for the children to share and enjoy with their families. One of the photocopiable sheets is a grid that lists activities relevant to the festivals most likely to be celebrated during the year.

While some of the photocopiable sheets can be coloured, children should also be encouraged to create their own designs whenever possible.

Using a wide range of resources

Most of the activities require only materials that should be readily available within your setting such as pencils, card and paper. Where reference is made to decorative or collage materials, examples might be given, but these can generally be substituted by an alternative. Be willing to

use the activities as starting points and adapt them to suit your needs and the materials available.

Other activities will suggest specific food relevant to a festival or culture. Most are available at major supermarkets. Indian sweets are referred to frequently. These are available in major cities such as in the East End of London and the Belgrave Road in Leicester which has many specialist shops. (A small amount goes a long way as they can be cut into small pieces.)

When choosing resources, it is essential that efforts are made to ensure that they do not contain stereotypical images. Be willing to discuss these images with the children and explain that they only show one aspect of the picture or that they might be out of date.

Links with home

Young children are more likely to achieve their own individual potential if the adults in their lives are working in partnership. Try to communicate the aims of activities to parents and carers and make efforts to include them wherever possible. Many families will be able to help by providing artefacts, examples of writing in different languages, singing, story-telling and so on. However, it would be wrong to assume that, because somebody comes from a particular background, they can read or write the language or know the background to particular festivals. Requests for assistance should be made sensitively.

When communicating with the children's families, be aware of the different structures that you might encounter – some children may have extended families while others might be in foster care. It is important to be aware of the children's individual backgrounds and not to make assumptions or judgements.

Learning in a multicultural world

Other books in this series have suggestions for multicultural links. This book is slightly different in that all of the activities start from a multicultural stance. Some activities are specific to a culture or religion while others include several cultures.

Children are easily influenced by the values of the adults who care for them. It is therefore important that an antiracist approach is developed from the beginning of their formal education.

Some people worry about attempting multicultural work because of the possibility of offending someone through lack of knowledge. There is no need to be concerned if you have an open mind, a willingness to find out and a positive attitude. The activities in this book should provide a useful starting point.

Some activities might lead to questions about race. Be willing to talk about the issues and make it clear to both children and adults that any indication of racism will not be tolerated.

Background to some popular festivals

Divali (October/November) is celebrated by Sikhs and Hindus throughout the world.

Hindus celebrate the return of Rama after 14 years in exile. He returned in darkness so the people lit divas (clay lamps) to welcome him home. It is a festival of light. Leicester's celebrations of Divali attract many people from all over Europe.

The Sikh story tells of Guru Gobind Singh who was released from prison at this time. The festival is celebrated with lights, fireworks, decorations and family gatherings. Hindus see it as the start of a new year when they balance their books and prepare for a new start. 'The story of Divali' is on the photocopiable sheets on pages 58 and 59.

Baisakhi (April) celebrates the start of the pure Sikh community in 1699. It is the day when Sikhs are baptised into their faith. The 'Five Ks' were introduced at this time. Baptised Sikhs wear these as a symbol of their faith – Kach (shorts); Kanga (comb); Kara (steel bracelet); Kesh (uncut hair) and Kirpan (sword). It is celebrated with family get-togethers and visits to the Gurdwara.

Easter (March/April) is the most important festival in the Christian year. It follows the period of repentance (Lent) and commemorates Jesus' death and resurrection. It is celebrated with the eating of Easter eggs – a symbol of new life.

Christmas (December) celebrates the birth of Jesus Christ. Many books have been written to tell the Christmas story.

Yuan Tan or **Chinese New Year** (January/February) is celebrated with fireworks, dancing and the giving of gifts. The colours gold and red are especially used in the decorations – red for luck and gold for prosperity.

The festival is associated with lion and dragon dancing. According to tradition, the years are named in the order in which 12 animals finished a race. 'The story of Chinese New Year' is on the photocopiable sheets on pages 61 and 62. People are said to take the characteristics of the animals according to the year in which they were born. For example, children born in the year 2000 should take the characteristics of the dragon and be emotional, eccentric, a good leader and prefer the night-time.

Eid-ul-Fitr (Winter) marks the end of Ramadan – a period of fasting. It is celebrated by visits to the Mosque, family meals and the sharing of sweets and cards.

Hanukkah (December) is a Jewish festival of light. It is celebrated with family meals and the lighting of a candle each night for eight days. 'The story of Hanukkah' is on the photocopiable sheet on page 63.

Rastafarian New Year (September) is celebrated with food, gatherings, exhibitions, music (especially drumming) and parties. The colours black, red, green and gold are symbolic.

Pesach or **Passover** (April) is a Jewish festival that celebrates the time when Moses led the Israelites from slavery in Egypt. It is celebrated with a meal in which all of the food is symbolic of the flight from Egypt.

Holi (March) is a Hindu festival which illustrates God's protection of believers. 'The story of Holi' is on the photocopiable sheet on page 57. It is celebrated with bonfires and the eating of roast coconut. In India, people play tricks on each other and wear old clothes so that they can throw coloured water over each other – a reminder of the playful activities of the young Lord Krishna.

Planning for individual needs
Young children need to feel confident to attempt new activities. It is important that raising the children's self-esteem is central to all planning. This should lead to a consideration of individual children's levels of development as well as the crucial elements of race, gender and disability.

This chapter has eight activities for encouraging personal, social and emotional development. There are activities that help the children to understand a range of cultures and festivals as well as activities that examine similarities and differences between people, and some that explore ways of caring for others.

Personal, social and emotional development

GROUP SIZE
Whole group.

TIMING
15 minutes.

HOME LINKS
Tell the children's parents and carers about the ideas that they had for being helpful to others. Ask them to support their child's efforts at home and help them by suggesting things that they can do such as fetching Grandma's spectacles or helping a younger sibling to do up their buttons.

FOLLOW-UP IDEAS
Display a list of the children's suggestions for being kind.

Make a big book of the story.

Dramatize the story with costumes and individual parts. Show the production to an audience.

THE GOOD SAMARITAN

Learning objective
To use a bible story to show the value of caring for all people.

What you need
Comfortable seating area; a children's bible.

Preparation
Familiarize yourself with the story of 'The Good Samaritan' – it can be found in Luke's Gospel, chapter 10, verse 29.

What to do
Sit in a circle with the children and say that you are going to tell a story about a good man who lived a long time ago. Explain that the Samaritan people and the Jewish people were not very friendly towards each other.

Tell the story about the good Samaritan in an interesting way. Retell it and invite individual children to stand in the centre of the circle and take the main parts. Together, talk about the different characters. Why do the children think they didn't stop to help? How do the children think they could be like the good Samaritan? Perhaps they could care for someone who has fallen over, or help tidy up.

Support
Simplify the story and encourage the children to suggest ways of being friends to each other.

Extension
Ask the children to think about how they can be kind to others and to try out their ideas.

CELEBRATION PARTIES

Learning objective
To celebrate special occasions from different faiths and cultures.

What you need
See the 'Celebration parties grid' on the photocopiable sheet on page 68.

What to do
Having parties is a fun and motivating way for young children to learn about different cultures. Below are some ideas for things to make and share to celebrate some popular festivals.

Chinese New Year
Share: Chinese sweets; prawn crackers; noodles.
Make: a blossom tree by decorating twigs with pink tissue flowers.

Holi
Share: biscuits decorated with icing and multicoloured cake decorations.
Make: splatter paintings – ensure that the area and the children are well-covered and place large sheets of paper on the floor. Splatter the paint to form colourful patterns.

Passover
Share: matzot.
Make: potato latkes by using the ingredients listed on the grid on page 68. Add the eggs, flour and salt to the potato and onion mixture. **NB** Heat the oil in a frying pan away from the children. Drop spoonfuls of the mixture into the oil and fry on both sides.

Easter
Share: chocolate nests. Mix breakfast cereal with melted chocolate, set in paper cake cases and put mini eggs on top.
Make: a tree from twigs and string (see the grid on page 68). Ask the children to decorate egg templates. Hang the eggs from the branches.

Eid
Share: Indian sweets such as barfi or jalebi.
Make: a star and crescent moon mobile. Help the children to make star and moon shapes from the provided materials (see the grid on page 68). Hang the shapes from the covered hoop.

Rastafarian New Year
Share: banana cake (the recipe is on page 69).
Make: use bright red, yellow and green paint to make patterns on pieces of black paper to decorate your room.

Divali
Share: Indian sweets.
Make: divas from play dough. Decorate in a variety of ways.

Hanukkah
Share: matzot.
Make: cards decorated with a hanukiah. Show the children a hanukiah. Ask them to draw one on a card. Let the children choose how to decorate their designs.

Support
Help the children with skills such as cutting and mixing.

Extension
Talk about the religious aspects of each festival and faith communitites.

THE THREE BUTTERFLIES

Learning objective
To use a story to talk about similarities and differences.

What you need
Red, yellow and blue coloured card; scrap materials in the same colours; glue; sticky tape; scissors; colouring materials; six short garden canes or pencils.

Preparation
Make one basic flower and butterfly shape of each colour and involve the children in decorating them. Attach them to the canes. Decorate card shapes to resemble the sun and the rain.

What to do
Use the props to tell the children the story of the butterflies, outlined below.

'Three different-coloured butterflies are playing together. It starts to rain. The red butterfly goes to the red flower for shelter. The flower welcomes the red butterfly but tells it that the other coloured butterflies may not come. The three butterflies then go to the other coloured flowers, but the yellow flower will only let the yellow butterfly stay and the blue flower will only let the blue butterfly stay. The butterflies decide to stay together even if they get wet. Eventually the rain passes and the sun returns.'

Talk to the children about how each and everyone is individual and different but how they still play and work together. Ask the children if they think it is fair to stop someone playing with them if they have for example, different-coloured hair or a different-coloured jumper. Explain that it is people's personalities that are important, not the clothes that they wear, or the way that they look.

Retell the story, this time asking the children to take the parts of the flowers, butterflies, rain and sun. Encourage them to use their own words and actions.

Support
Tell the story a second time and invite the children to hold up the props at the appropriate times.

Extension
Encourage the children to dramatize the whole story. Extend the discussion and be willing to discuss skin colour with the children.

Small groups.

Five to ten minutes.

PEACE AND QUIET

Learning objective
To learn about the importance of quiet reflective times.

What you need
A quiet comfortable area; a focal point such as a vase of flowers or a peaceful picture; a large piece of paper; a thick pen.

What to do
Ask the children to sit quietly and comfortably – they will need their own space so that they are not disturbed or distracted. Show them the focal point and ask them to look at it very carefully.

Explain that people called Buddhist monks live very thoughtful and peaceful lives in special buildings called monasteries around the world – there are several of these monasteries in Britain. Buddhist monks try to put others first, work hard and care for all living things. Every year, they have a time when they go to stay somewhere very quiet and peaceful where they spend a lot of time thinking. At the end of this time, they are presented with new robes to wear. This special day is called Kathina Day and in England it happens in the autumn.

Explain that you would like the children to sit quietly and think about some of the things that they have done recently. What things did they do well? What things could they have done better? After they have thought for a little while, ask them to put up their hands and tell you about one of the things that they thought about. Write their thoughts down onto a large piece of paper.

Explain to parents and carers that it is important for children to have quiet times during the day and encourage them to find a time for reflection together.

Use music such as Beethoven's *Moonlight Sonata* to create a feeling of peace.

Establish a permanent quiet area in your room.

Support
Ask the children more specific questions to help them to remember something that they have recently enjoyed or done well.

Extension
Encourage the children to reflect more on their relationships with others than on specific activities. Ask them to think of one particular way in which they can improve a friendship – perhaps by letting a friend join a game or sharing something with them.

SIX BLIND MEN

Learning objective
To learn to listen to each other's points of view.

What you need
A large piece of paper; a marker pen; thick and thin card; old tights; thick rope; double-sided tape; newspaper; scissors; corrugated card; blindfold; an adult helper; the poem 'The wise men and the elephant' on the photocopiable sheet on page 66.

Preparation
Draw a large elephant onto the piece of paper. Make a 3-D trunk from old tights stuffed with newspaper. Cut pointed tusks from thick card. Make an ear from card, slightly folded in the middle to make a fan shape. Curve the corrugated card and fill with newspaper to form a leg. Attach all the pieces to produce an elephant with different textures. Add the rope for the tail.

What to do
Choose six children who have not seen the elephant to leave the room with your helper. Ask the helper to bring in the children, one at a time, blindfolded. Ask them to feel a part of the elephant and guess what it is. Encourage the children to use descriptive language as they feel the elephant's floppy ears or bendy trunk. Each child will probably think that the elephant is something different – perhaps a tree trunk, a snake, a spear, a fan or a rope. When all the children have had a turn, show them the complete elephant. Talk together about how everyone had different ideas. Explain how it is important to listen to each other's ideas to build up the whole picture of something. Finish by reading the poem 'The wise men and the elephant' on the photocopiable sheet on page 66.

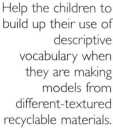

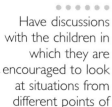

Support
Some children may not be happy about wearing a blindfold. Place a cloth over the picture and guide their hands underneath.

Extension
Extend the discussion about considering different points of view with the children, such as in disagreements over a toy or by looking at a story from the point of view of a different character. For example, how did the troll feel when the goats went over his bridge?

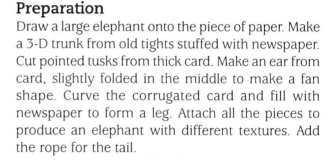

RULES

Learning objective
To understand the need to have rules and to develop a set of group rules.

What you need
Easel or flip chart; pens.

What to do
Ask the children what they understand by the word 'rules'. Explain that rules are things that people must follow so that everyone can live happily together. Look at some different examples of rules together. Tell the children about Ramadan. Explain that during this special time, adult Muslims have a rule where they are not allowed to eat during daylight hours and they must spend lots of time thinking and praying. Tell the children that this is a very important part of their religion (it is one of the compulsory Five Pillars of Islam) and although it is difficult, adult Muslims try hard to keep the rules.

Ask the children to think about rules that they have to keep at home or in the group. Ask the children for some ideas of rules for the group. Write down their suggestions on a flip chart. Try to keep the rules positive and ensure that they all start with 'do', rather than 'don't'. Encourage all the children to contribute.

Support
Start by talking about rules at home. Children may think of things such as taking off muddy shoes or putting toys away.

Extension
Talk about rules in games with the children. What would happen if there were no rules? Ask them to describe some rules for a simple game such as 'Snakes and ladders'.

Ask parents and carers to talk with their child about the rules that they have at home. Give parents and carers the opportunity to talk to you about any worries that they may have about their child's behaviour at home. Find out about behaviour management courses for carers, which might be provided by a local school, community education group or social services.

Decorate your list of rules and display them in your room.

• • • • • •

Talk about other religious rules that might affect families.

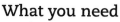

MAKING JUDGEMENTS

Learning objective
To learn to think carefully before making a judgement.

What you need
A selection of 'exotic' fruits such as pawpaw, mango, pineapple and passion fruit; passion fruit juice; a knife to cut the fruit; paper cups.

What to do
Examine the fruits by feeling, smelling, listening and looking. Encourage the children to use descriptive language as they examine the fruits. Which fruits do they like best and least? Why did they choose those particular fruits? Look at the wrinkled exterior of the passion fruit. Did the children choose that one? Cut the fruits in half and repeat the discussion. Are the choices still the same? Did the children change their opinion of the passion fruit? It is far more interesting inside.

Now give the children a taste of passion fruit juice. What do they think now? Talk about how they perhaps did not like the look of the passion fruit, yet they changed their mind when they tasted it. Have the children ever changed their mind about something in this way before – perhaps when they tried another kind of food?

Support
Some children might need encouragement to taste new foods. Extend their use of descriptive language during the discussion with words such as wrinkled, prickly, smooth and sweet.

Extension
Make a list of all the describing words that the children used. Talk in greater depth about judging people by their appearances. It is easy to judge people based on what they look like on the outside, but is this always the right thing to do?

GROUP SIZE
Ten to 12 children.

TIMING
Ten minutes.

HOME LINKS
Ask parents and carers to talk to their child about making choices and doing the right thing.

FOLLOW-UP IDEAS
Make up stories together in which good triumphs over evil.
• • • • • •
Celebrate the festival concerned with cards, decorations and a party.
• • • • • •
List the 'good' and 'bad' actions in the story.

DOING THE RIGHT THING

Learning objective

To learn about the stories of Divali and Holi and how good triumphs in them.

What you need

'The story of Holi' on the photocopiable sheet on page 57; 'The story of Divali' on the photocopiable sheets on pages 58 and 59; simple props or masks to represent the main characters in the stories – such as a pot, a cloak for a king, a tail for a monkey, a trunk for an elephant and flame-coloured tissue strips to wear on the wrist for fire.

Preparation

Make the props and masks.

What to do

Tell the children the Hindu story of either Holi (in the spring) or Divali (in the autumn). Adapt the language in the story to suit the age of your children. Both stories provide plenty of scope for the children to act out. As you read them, you will be able to allocate parts which can be determined by simple costumes, puppets or masks. Retell the story with the children joining in at appropriate times. Talk about the way good triumphs in the end and discuss how it is always best to do the right thing.

Support

The children might prefer to use a mask on a stick rather than one that goes around their face. Talk about times when it is difficult to do the right thing.

Extension

Talk about the feelings of the main characters in the story and relate these to times when the children have had to make choices.

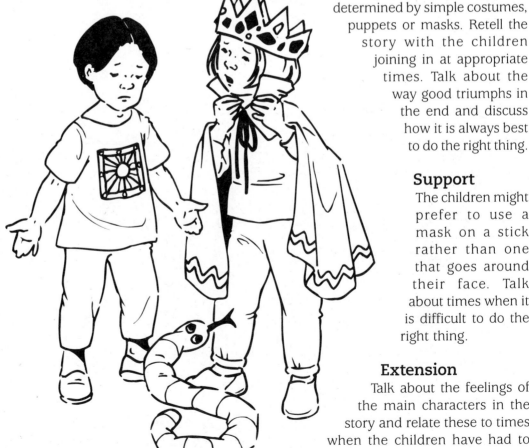

This chapter has eight activities covering a range of skills in this area of learning. Story-telling traditions are explored in tales from around the world, such as the Anansi stories and the children are introduced to dual language books. Other activities include pencil-control skills, early writing development and rhymes in more than one language are enjoyed.

GROUP SIZE
Whole group or small groups.

TIMING
Ten minutes a day.

HOME LINKS
Ask parents and carers to send in books that they might have or, even better, ask if they will tell their own traditional stories to the children.

FOLLOW-UP IDEAS
Listen to the music and taste some food from the country concerned. Add other materials from the country to the display.

• • • • • •

Talk about the illustrations in the book. What do they tell us about the country of origin?

Communication, language and literacy

STORIES ON DISPLAY

Learning objective
To listen to stories set in other cultures.

What you need
A quiet and comfortable area; a story such as *Handa's Surprise* by Eileen Browne (Walker); a display area; a globe (optional).

Preparation
Become familiar with the story, find out a little bit about the country of origin and prepare a display area – any size from a small space on a shelf upwards.

What to do
Explain to the children that you are going to read a story from a particular country. Tell them that stories are enjoyed by children everywhere.

If appropriate, show the children where it is on a globe and give them some details of the place. These should be as accurate as possible, avoiding stereotypical descriptions. For example, Africa is often illustrated as having villages of round houses, little water and poverty. While these exist in some parts of Africa, such an image ignores the variety of countries, landscapes, languages and cultures that make up the continent of 'Africa'. After reading *Handa's Surprise* to the children, place the book in a special place reserved to display the books. Add to this as other stories are told.

Support
Refer to other pictures and books that are available to show the children a little of what life is like in another country.

Extension
Encourage the children to find out more about the country of the story using information books. Talk about the way that story-telling traditions are passed on.

GROUP SIZE
Whole or small groups.

TIMING
Ten minutes.

HOME LINKS
Ask parents and carers to help their child to search for examples on food packets. Can any of the parents and carers demonstrate writing in different languages? Invite them to share this skill with their child.

READ ALL ABOUT IT

Learning objective
To find examples of different languages.

What you need
Examples of different languages in print taken from food packaging, instructions to electrical items, newspapers and so on; display area and backing materials.

Preparation
Cut out the samples and prepare the display area.

What to do
Start by talking about how written words tell us things. Look at items printed in English. What do the children notice? Do they recognize any of the letters? Look at the examples written in different languages and ask the same questions. Encourage the children to find the similarities and differences between the languages. Let individual children tell the group about their personal experiences of different languages.

Mount the samples of different languages and use them to form a wall or table display. Ask the children for suggestions for labels, for example, 'Leon's writing tells the ingredients of the biscuits in *Arabic*'. Include the name of the language and where it was found. Where possible, include the English translation.

Support
Start by encouraging the children to recognize the difference between words and pictures in their favourite story-books. Show them some examples of stories written in another language, or dual-language texts if they are available. Talk about the shapes of the letters together.

FOLLOW-UP IDEAS
Encourage the children to listen to examples of different languages. Libraries sometimes stock tapes of stories that would be suitable.

Try to learn a rhyme, poem or song in a different language.

Continue to look for examples of different languages throughout the year.

Extension
Let the children choose their favourite piece of text and allow them to experiment at copying the shapes and direction of the letters.

Involve the children in writing or decorating the labels and mounting the examples for the display.

Rice

चावल

Riz

ANANSI STORIES

Learning objective
To learn about story-telling traditions and how stories have arrived from other cultures.

What you need
A book containing an Anansi story such as 'From Tiger to Anansi' by Philip Sherlock in *The Fairy Tale Treasury* (Puffin).

Preparation
Familiarize yourself with the story.

What to do
Explain to the children that you would like to tell them a story about Anansi. Tell the children that it is traditional for Anansi stories to be told rather than read straight from the book. After you have told the story, talk about the style of the story. Explain that the Anansi stories have come from a different country – they came from West Africa many years ago. People from there were kidnapped and taken to the Caribbean to work, but they remembered their stories and took them with them. Later, when people from the Caribbean moved to the United Kingdom, the stories travelled too, and that is how we can hear them today.

Support
Simplify and explain the story as necessary. Talk about stories that the children would like to take with them if they travelled.

Extension
Use a map or globe to plot the route of the stories.

GROUP SIZE

GROUP SIZE
Five to 12 children.

TIMING
20 minutes.

HOME LINKS
Suggest that parents and carers help their child to search for minibeasts under stones, in walls, paving cracks and bark. Ask them to explain that they must always put the creature back in their homes and that they must not harm them.

FOLLOW-UP IDEAS
Talk about the different places that creatures live in.

· · · · · ·

Make a colourful display of the banyan tree, and ask the children to draw and attach the creatures at the appropriate places in the tree. Take the opportunity to use positional words such as *in*, *on*, *among*, *under* and *through*.

· · · · · ·

Try to look at the story from both points of view – the woodcutter who was following instructions, and the animals protecting their homes.

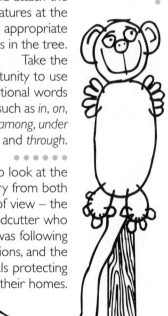

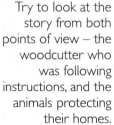

THE BANYAN TREE

Learning objective
To use puppets to retell a story.

What you need
'The story of the banyan tree' on the photocopiable sheet on page 60; clean, lolly sticks or short canes (old pencils or rolled paper could be used as a substitute); thin card; colouring materials; pencils; scissors; sticky tape.

Preparation
Prepare the area for a story and a craft activity.

What to do
Gather the children together and explain that you are going to tell a story about a tree that is the home to many animals. Ask the children to listen carefully as they will be joining in with the story later.

Read the story to the children and talk about it together. What would have happened to the animals if the tree had been chopped down? Would it be right for someone to cut down a tree that belonged to everyone?

Invite the children to draw and cut out one of the main characters or animals. Attach the children's drawings to sticks to make stick puppets. There should be enough of each creature for all the children to be involved.

Retell the story, with the children taking the parts of the animals and a child playing the part of the woodcutter.

As the story is told, encourage each group of animals to join in at the appropriate part.

Support
Provide additional support to make the puppets, particularly with attaching the picture to the stick. Encourage the children to take an active part in the story-telling.

Extension
Talk about how the creatures in the story feel when they think they are at risk of losing their homes. Ask the children to think of their own ending to the story.

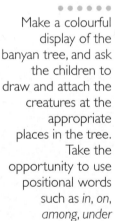

BILINGUAL BOOKS

Learning objective
To read and enjoy stories from bilingual books.

What you need
A comfortable area; a selection of bilingual books such as the *Spot* books by Eric Hill (Puffin) and *It's Mine* by Rod Campbell (Puffin). Mantra and Magi publish a range of bilingual books and others are available in libraries.

What to do
Sit with the children and establish an air of anticipation before the story. Remove any distractions and try to engage the children's enthusiasm and interest for sharing a new story. Explain that the story that you are going to share is a special one, because it is written in two languages – English and another language. Why do the children think that it is written in two languages? Do any of the children speak more than one language? Do they know anyone that does? Show them the print on the pages and point out the two different types of writing.

Read the story in English to the children but also help them to understand that other languages are as important and useful as their own. Explain that there are many people who can speak, read and write in several languages. If possible, invite someone who can read the language to share the session with you, so that the children can relate the spoken word to the text.

Support
Show the book to small groups of children at a time and let them look closely at the two different types of word. Point to the words as you read them the English version.

Extension
Let the children draw parts of the story and write out a caption in one of the languages.

GROUP SIZE

GROUP SIZE
Small groups.

TIMING
Ten minutes.

HOME LINKS
Ask parents and carers to practise other action rhymes at home with their child and to listen to the new versions. Encourage them to learn the new version of the rhyme from their child.

FOLLOW-UP IDEAS
Find other rhymes to learn in different languages, such as 'Frère Jacques'.

● ● ● ● ● ●

Display a large picture of a person. Label it in English and at least one other language.

● ● ● ● ● ●

Listen out for rhyming words in the children's favourite nursery rhymes, such as 'Jill' and 'hill' in 'Jack and Jill'.

RHYME TIME

Learning objective
To learn a rhyme in a different language.

What you need
A familiar rhyme, with the words in a different language (see Preparation, below).

Preparation
Choose a simple, familiar rhyme such as 'Head, Shoulders, Knees and Toes' and find out the words in a different language. You may find them by looking in a dual language dictionary, or perhaps a parent or carer or another member of staff will be able to help you.

What to do
Ask the children to stand in a space to give them room to perform the actions. Teach the children the song and the actions for 'Head, Shoulders, Knees and Toes' using the English version. When they are confident with this, introduce the names of the parts of the body in a different language. Start with just head and shoulders then gradually add the others. Continue the actions to reinforce the words. Encourage all of the children in the group to join in.

Support
Practise the rhyme over the course of several sessions. Allow the children to take their time to familiarize themselves with the English version before introducing the next language. Slow the pace when learning the new words and learn a few at a time. Enjoy practising the actions together to reinforce the rhyme.

Extension
Suggest that older children perfect the actions and the words for both versions and encourage them to perform the rhymes for a group performance.

GROUP SIZE
Five or six children.

TIMING
20 minutes.

HOME LINKS
Send the completed pictures home with the children. Ask parents and carers to look for the items when they take their child shopping.

FOLLOW-UP IDEAS

Go for a walk to the shops. Look for labelling and pricing – especially at the greengrocer's.

• • • • • •

Write labels for objects in the room. Use initial sounds and pictures to help the children to recognize them. Play games with the labels so that they are referred to regularly.

• • • • • •

Set up your role-play area as a shop with labelled items to sell.

NAME THAT FRUIT!

Learning objective
To label the items on a fruit and vegetable stall.

What you need
A copy of the photocopiable sheet 'Market stall' on page 70 for each child; real fruit and vegetables or pictures cut from magazines; scissors; glue; colouring materials.

Preparation
Make a display of the fruit and vegetables (and pictures).

What to do
Ask the children to tell you about a time when they went to buy fruit and vegetables with an adult. Did they go to a greengrocer's shop, a market or a big supermarket? What do they remember about their trip? Can they describe what they saw or smelled? Together, discuss the sights, sounds and smells that they experienced.

Now give each child a copy of the photocopiable sheet and talk to

the children about the fruits and vegetables they can see on the market stall. Show them any examples or pictures that you might have. What names do the children call the different fruits and vegetables? Read out the names on the labels on the sheet. Have a look at the spaces for the labels on the market stall. Work as a group to decide where the labels should be placed. Cut out the labels and stick them in the correct places. Colour the fruit and vegetables in appropriate colours.

Support
Help cut out the labels for the children and read the label for them, emphasizing the initial sound.

Extension
Encourage the children to make drawings of other fruit and vegetables and to write appropriate labels for them.

GROUP SIZE
Five or six children.

TIMING
15 minutes.

PENCIL PATTERNS

Learning objective
To develop pencil-control skills by copying patterns from a variety of cultures.

What you need
A large piece of paper; a marker pen; board or easel; individual pieces of paper; sharp pencils; the photocopiable sheet 'Patterns' on page 71.

Preparation
Place the paper and pencils on a table close to the board or easel. Make an enlarged copy of the photocopiable sheet.

HOME LINKS
Give parents and carers examples of the patterns and ask them to help their child to practise left to right movements when making marks on a page.

What to do
Show the children the enlarged photocopiable sheet with the patterns on it and talk about the patterns together. Do the children recognize any of them? Help them to describe the patterns and to draw them in the air with a finger.

Choose one of the simple patterns from the sheet and draw it onto a large sheet of paper (or the board). Talk the children through the pattern as you make it, describing the strokes of your pen. Show them how to take care when making the strokes and explain that it is important to concentrate and take your time when making a pattern.

Before writing, ensure that the children are comfortably seated with a sharpened pencil. Help them to hold the pencil correctly – this will be easier if it is a comfortable size and shape. Provide pencil grips, if necessary. Encourage the children to continue the pattern to the end. Talk to them about starting at the top and working from left to right.

FOLLOW-UP IDEAS
Trace some shapes and simple pictures.

• • • • • •

Continue the pattern work in art activities, for example by finger-painting the patterns.

• • • • • •

Look for patterns in everyday surroundings and suggest that the children try to copy them.

Support
Let the children begin with straight patterns across a large sheet of paper. Use a variety of colours and types of writing implement, such as pencils, crayons and chalks.

Extension
Gradually make the patterns smaller and more varied for the children. Begin to introduce actual letters.

The eight activities in this chapter concentrate on mathematical development. The children will have opportunities to develop sequencing and ordering skills and will learn about number rhymes in other languages, as well as perfecting their counting skills as they count the number of candles on a menorah and count down the days to Christmas.

Mathematical development

GROUP SIZE
Small groups.

TIMING
15 minutes.

HOME LINKS
Ask parents and carers to provide examples of different numbers for the display if possible. Ask them to help their child to practise counting sets of five objects at home.

FOLLOW-UP IDEAS
Look for other examples of writing in different languages.

• • • • • •

Learn a number rhyme in a different language.

• • • • • •

Make and use a number line up to five.

NUMBER SYSTEMS

Learning objective
To make a display and discuss different ways of writing.

What you need
Examples of the numerals 1 to 5 in different cultures (a Punjabi/English frieze of the numbers 1 to 10 is available from the Minority Group Support Services in Coventry, tel: 02476-717800); pictures of sets of five objects; display space; backing paper.

Preparation
Try to find out the pronunciation of some numbers from a different language. Prepare the display material.

What to do
Count from 1 to 5 in English with the children, pointing to the numbers on a large piece of paper or mural as you speak. Now show them the numbers in another language or script. If known, try pronouncing the numbers in this language, inviting the children to join in and copy you. Talk about the language used and the way in which numbers are formed. Show the children how the numbers are written from left to right in a line across the page.

Write the numbers from 1 to 5 in the air with your finger and encourage the children to join in. Emphasize how in English writing, we start drawing numbers from the top to the bottom.

Make a display of the numbers from 1 to 5, showing the English numbers and examples from other cultures. Ask the children to draw some numbers of their own choice to add to the display. Add the name of the language close to the example. Add sets of five items either drawn by the group or cut from magazines and catalogues. Count them as they are added to the display.

Support
Help the children to count to five, ensuring that they point to each number or object, using one-to-one correspondence as they count.

Extension
Extend the activity for the children to look at numbers to ten.

GROUP SIZE
Five or six children.

TIMING
Ten minutes.

HOME LINKS
Give each child a copy of the photocopiable sheet 'Finish the shapes' on page 72 and ask them to finish the patterns and pictures with their parents and carers.

FOLLOW-UP IDEAS
Make a collection of symmetrical objects in the room.

• • • • • •

Look at Islamic patterns and talk about the various examples of symmetry.

• • • • • •

Divide a rectangular or circular piece of paper into two.

• • • • • •

Make 'blob' pictures by putting a 'blob' of wet paint in the middle of a piece of paper. Fold the paper in half and press gently. Open to find a symmetrical shape.

SYMMETRICAL SHAPES

Learning objective
To explore the properties of a variety of shapes.

What you need
An unbreakable mirror for each child; a selection of symmetrical shapes cut from thin card – include some that have a connection with different faith and cultural groups such as stars, crescent moons, bells, lotus flowers, crosses and so on; the photocopiable sheets 'Patterns' on page 71 and 'Finish the shapes' on page 72.

Preparation
Build up the collection of shapes (some are shown on the photocopiable sheet on page 71). Draw the line of symmetry on one side of each shape.

What to do
Show the children the collection of shapes and symbols and tell them something about each one. Show the children how to place the mirror on top of one of the shapes to get a reflection that makes the shape whole again. Explain that this sort of shape is called symmetrical, but not all shapes are like this. Let them each have a turn to hold the mirror along the line of symmetry.

Let the children experiment with some other shapes, holding the mirror along the lines marked on them. What things do they find out? Can they describe what they see? What happens if they put the mirror in a different place?

Support
Use a selection of paper shapes and ask the children to try to fold them along the pre-drawn lines of symmetry, rather than using the mirrors.

Extension
Use the side of the shapes without a line drawn on so that the children need to find their own line of symmetry. Provide extra shapes that are not symmetrical for the children to explore. Ask the children to sort the shapes into two sets – symmetrical and unsymmetrical. Talk about objects around them that are symmetrical such as the cross on the first-aid box or shapes in a construction set.

GROUP SIZE
Small groups.

TIMING
20 minutes.

HOME LINKS
Ask parents and carers to help their child to learn the months of the year in a fun way, by remembering events that have happened or by learning when significant birthdays are – 'Remember Mummy's birthday is in July when it is the summer but your birthday is in the winter, just after Christmas'.

FOLLOW-UP IDEAS
Make a similar circle for the four seasons.

• • • • • •

Make a timeline of the year including photographs of the children (with parental consent) in the months of their birth.

CIRCLE OF LIFE

Learning objective
To become familiar with the cycle of the year.

What you need
A long strip of thin card, approximately 120cm x 12cm; drawing and colouring materials; glue; magazines, brochures and postcards to cut up (with suitable pictures of different times of the year); the photocopiable sheet 'Around the year' on page 73 (containing pictures of some festivals that can be cut up).

Preparation
Fold the strip of card into 12 divisions.

What to do
Talk to the children about the months of the year – their names and what happens during the year, for example when we have holidays or festivals, such as Christmas, Baisakhi and Hanukkah; when the leaves fall from the trees and when trees and flowers show new growth. Write the names of the months on the different sections of the card.

Suggest a different month to each child and help them to think of a picture to make to represent the month. Remind the children of the features of the months and the festivals at that time. Let them draw their own picture or cut one out from the magazines, cards, brochures or photocopiable sheet.

Show the children how the strip of card can be joined to make a circle and discuss how the yearly circle goes round and round with no beginning or ending. Explain that the Buddha taught about the Cycle of Life being represented by the Wheel of Life. The Wheel is one of the symbols of Buddhism.

Support
Provide the children with plenty of support when they are choosing a picture. Remind them of activities that they might have done at different times of the year. Encourage them to learn the date of their birthday and other special dates in their lives.

Extension
Ask the children to remember activities and encourage them to take a more active part in the discussion. Help them to learn to recognize the names of the months of the year in the correct order.

GROUP SIZE
Whole group.

TIMING
Five minutes per day from
1 December.

HOME LINKS
Ask the children to talk to their parents and carers about the preparations that they are making. Encourage them to open an Advent calendar at home each day. Children whose families do not celebrate Christmas can look for similarities and differences in preparation for other events.

FOLLOW-UP IDEAS
Talk about how Jesus was born in a stable. Remind the children that it is the giving of gifts that is important – not the cost.

• • • • • •

Find out about the celebration of Christmas in different parts of the world.

• • • • • •

Make an Advent wreath.

ADVENT CANDLE

Learning objective
To develop number recognition, counting and ordering skills.

What you need
A large cardboard roll such as from aluminium foil, kitchen roll or wrapping paper; piece of white paper; flame-coloured tissue paper; glue; scissors; cardboard base; thick felt-tipped pens; fir cones or alternative decoration for the base.

Preparation
Cover the roll in the white paper and attach this to the cardboard base. Mark it in 24 numbered stripes or bands to indicate the number of days until Christmas. Decorate the base with cones or an alternative seasonal idea such as holly. Make the tissue into a 'flame' and attach to the top of the paper-covered roll to look like a candle.

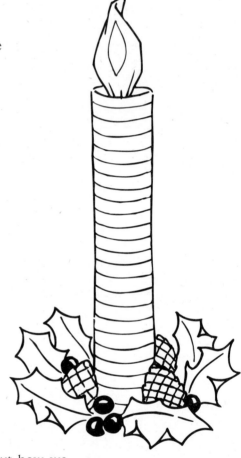

What to do
Talk to the children about how we wait for Christmas to come. What things do people do to get ready for Christmas? What do we do at the group? At home? At church? In the shops? Talk about making the cake, decorating shop windows, writing to Father Christmas and practising for the Nativity play. How do the children feel? Do they get excited?

Invite a different child to colour in a strip each day, starting at the top. Together, count down the days to Christmas.

Support
Help the children to count backwards by using a simple number line, chart or pile of interlocking cubes.

Extension
Let the children have their own individual candle calendars – either smaller versions of the above or drawn on paper. Encourage older children to think about preparations in other parts of the world. How do people prepare in hot countries? What are the similarities and differences?

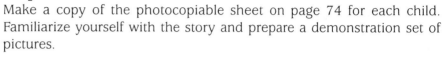

GROUP SIZE
Small groups.

TIMING
20 minutes.

HOME LINKS
Ask parents and carers to help their child to understand and use the words first, next and last at home. For example, when laying the table – first we put the cloth on, next the plates and last of all, the cutlery.

FOLLOW-UP IDEAS
Act out the different scenes of the story.

• • • • • •

Explain how the festival is celebrated with games, playing jokes, throwing coloured water and sharing foods such as pakoras and samosas.

• • • • • •

Divide other familiar stories or nursery rhymes into scenes and sequence them.

PICTURE STORY

Learning objective

To develop sequencing and ordering skills.

What you need

The photocopiable sheet 'Holi pictures' on page 74; 'The story of Holi' on the photocopiable sheet on page 57; glue; scissors; colouring materials; paper.

Preparation

Make a copy of the photocopiable sheet on page 74 for each child. Familiarize yourself with the story and prepare a demonstration set of pictures.

What to do

Tell the children the Hindu story of Holi on the photocopiable sheet on page 57. Talk about the different parts of the story together and discuss how it can be broken down into sections: the young prince and the king; the prince and the potter praying for the kittens; the snakes in the pit; the elephants in the grass; the soldiers with their swords; and the bonfire.

Show the children your pre-prepared pictures. Talk about what each picture shows and try to decide which of the pictures comes first, second and so on.

Provide each child with their own copy of the photocopiable sheet on page 74 and ask them to cut the pictures out and put them in the order of the story. Use the opportunity to develop the appropriate vocabulary – first, second, last and so on. When the children are happy with the order of the pictures, show them how to stick them into place on a piece of paper. Encourage them to colour in the pictures and to use them to retell their own version of the story.

Support

Help the children to cut out the pictures. Retell the story as the children place the pictures in order, encouraging them to recall what happened next.

Extension

Ask the children to add further scenes to the story by drawing more pictures in the sequence.

GROUP SIZE
12 children.

TIMING
20 minutes.

HOME LINKS
Encourage parents and carers to help their child to use and understand ordinal numbers by using the words in everyday situations such as, What colour is the next car to go past? Find the second page. Who came first?

FOLLOW-UP IDEAS
Find out more about the way that the Chinese New Year is celebrated.

• • • • • •

Use ordinal numbers at every opportunity such as when lining up or when finishing drinks. Help the children to realize that finishing first is not always best.

ORDINAL NUMBERS

Learning objective
To use the Chinese New Year story to become familiar with ordinal numbers.

What you need
'The story of Chinese New Year' on the photocopiable sheets on pages 61 and 62; colouring materials; scissors; Blu-Tack; a large piece of paper or whiteboard; small pieces of drawing paper for each child.

Preparation
Familiarize yourself with the story on pages 61 and 62 and prepare a large sketch of the river banks in the story on paper or a whiteboard. Space the river banks far enough apart for the children to add pictures of the animals in the story.

What to do
Tell the children 'The story of Chinese New Year'. Allocate each child one of the twelve animals to draw. Cut out the finished animal pictures.

Show the children the large picture of the river banks. Retell the story with the children joining in where they can. As each animal finishes the race, ask the children to use Blu-Tack to fix their animal to the picture behind the previous animal, so that they are in the correct order.

When the picture is complete, talk about what you have made. Encourage the children to use ordinal numbers to describe the order of the animals in the race. Ask them questions such as, 'Who came first, second, fifth?' and so on. Invite individual children to select an animal and then come out and count from the front to find out what position the animal came – 'I chose the snake, he came fifth in the race'.

Support
Talk about the names of the animals and the ways in which they normally move. Help the children to place the animals in the correct order. Supply simple line drawings of the animals for the children to colour in.

Extension
Choose an animal and ask the children to tell you how many are in front and behind.

HANUKKAH COUNTING

Learning objective

To develop forward and backward counting skills.

What you need

'The story of Hanukkah' on the photocopiable sheet on page 63; the
photocopiable sheet 'A special menorah' on page 75; paper for each child;
colouring materials; glue; scissors; red, yellow and
orange tissue paper.

Preparation

Prepare the area for a story and a
craft activity.

What to do

Read the children 'The story of
Hanukkah' on page 63 and talk
about the ways that the festival
is celebrated. One way is to have
a special menorah which has a
server flame and eight others.
One light is added each day until
all eight are burning.

Ask the children to draw around the
fingers on both hands (not the thumbs)
leaving a small space in the middle of the
two hands. Draw the 'slave' candle in this space.
Add a base to make it look like a menorah.

Let the children use red, yellow and orange tissue paper to add a flame
to their picture every day. When adding the flames, use mathematical
language to ask questions such as, How many flames are there? How
many more do we need? How many will there be tomorrow? Use the
vocabulary more, less, before and after and use the flames to practise
counting forwards and backwards – saying the name of the number as
each flame is touched.

Support

Make sure that the counting activity
and the language you use is
appropriate to the individual
children. Help the children to
make the menorah by
holding the paper still as
they draw around their
fingers.

Extension

Make a mistake as you
count the candles and see if
the children can spot it. Begin
counting in 2s with the adult
counting 1, 3, 5, 7 and the children
filling in the missing numbers.

NUMBER RHYMES

Learning objectives

To become familiar with a rhyme from a different culture and to recognize similarities across rhymes.

What you need

Three cards with 1st, 2nd and 3rd written on them in bold print; props to illustrate hens (optional); the photocopiable sheet 'Rhyme time' on page 67.

HOME LINKS
Send home a copy of the words so that the children can perform the rhyme with their families. Invite parents and carers to come in to share any number rhymes that they know in different languages.

FOLLOW-UP IDEAS
Learn another song in the same or a different language.

Link the rhyme to 'The story of Chinese New Year' on pages 61 and 62 in which the animals finished the race in first, second and third positions.

What to do

Learn a number rhyme in English – particularly one that can be dramatized or has actions such as 'Five Currant Buns' (Traditional). Next listen to a rhyme in another language such as the one on the photocopiable sheet on page 67.

Learn to sing the French version and say the English one. Allocate parts to the children and together do actions and dramatize both language versions of the rhyme. Let the children playing the part of the hens hold up the appropriate cards at the relevant points of the rhyme.

Now divide the group into two and perform both rhymes alternately. Explain to the children that although the rhymes are in different languages they both say the same thing, and talk about first, second and third. You could also explain that, just as they learn to count with number rhymes, some French children learn about numbers with this rhyme.

Support

Let the children enjoy listening to the new words and encourage them to join in with the actions.

Extension

Draw a picture, either individually or as a group and write first, second and third, in English and French, in the appropriate places.

In this chapter, the children will enjoy developing their knowledge and understanding of the world through these eight activities. They will find out where food comes from, make a traditional Caribbean banana cake and use their senses to explore products that represent multicultural Britain today.

Knowledge and understanding of the world

GROUP SIZE
Five to six children.

TIMING
Ten minutes.

HOME LINKS
Ask parents and carers to help collect labels from other countries. Invite any visitors who have lived overseas to talk to the children about living there.

FOLLOW-UP IDEAS
Find out more about the countries of origin using information books.

Arrange to visit a supermarket and look at the labels on the packaging.

WHERE IN THE WORLD?

Learning objective
To make a collection of food labels and talk about where they came from.

What you need
World map; paper for lists; thick felt-tipped pens; labels from food packaging stating the country of origin; display area and materials.

Preparation
Cut out the labels and packaging ready for use.

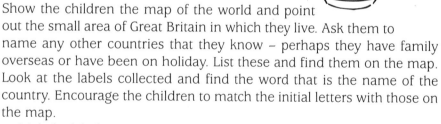

What to do
Show the children the map of the world and point out the small area of Great Britain in which they live. Ask them to name any other countries that they know – perhaps they have family overseas or have been on holiday. List these and find them on the map. Look at the labels collected and find the word that is the name of the country. Encourage the children to match the initial letters with those on the map.

Stick the labels onto a piece of paper – a separate one for each country. Place these on the appropriate parts of the map. Talk about the way that countries buy and sell things from each other, explaining, for example, that we buy fruit from New Zealand and sell cars to France.

Support
Talk in more general terms to the children about the different countries of the world and the produce that they are famous for.

Extension
Refer to the map in other sessions with the children, such as when different countries are mentioned in story-books.

GROUP SIZE
Small groups.

TIMING
Ten minutes.

HOME LINKS
Ask parents and carers to make a contribution to the role-play area – particularly items which need not be returned, such as greeting cards or newspapers. Invite parents and carers to play with the children in the role-play area.

SPECIAL PLACE

Learning objective
To set up the role-play area in ways that incorporate different cultures and customs.

What you need
Collection of artefacts, pictures and books from a range of cultures.

What to do
Make collections of artefacts that represent different cultures present in Britain. Ideas include:

Caribbean – paintings of Caribbean children, mounted like photographs; food such as tinned mango and guava; Caribbean music; dolls dressed in black with red, gold and green trimming.

India and Pakistan – religious artefacts such as Divali and Eid cards; dressing-up clothes; wedding invitations; books in relevant languages; pictures.

Italy – pictures from Italy; books about Italy; food such as pasta or pizza.

When including these artefacts in the area, it is important to avoid stereotyping. The home corner can stay as it is, with small suggestions to indicate different groups, or a café could include a menu of dishes to reflect different cultures.

Discuss the area with the children and involve them in making decisions about what should be included. For a café, talk about which pictures should be on the wall. Should the table-cloths reflect the colours of the flag and which languages should be included on the signs?

Support
Show the children how to use the artefacts that might be new to them. Play with them for short periods to introduce vocabulary and discuss the new items.

Extension
Explain to the children that although some items are new to them, this does not mean that they are 'strange' or 'funny'. Find out more about the country and why particular items are used.

FOLLOW-UP IDEAS
Take the children shopping to buy materials for the area to give them a sense of involvement.

Hold story-telling and cookery sessions relevant to the culture represented in the role-play area.

Decorate the area with materials relevant to a particular festival, for example, include red and gold paper decorations for Chinese New Year.

GROUP SIZE
Small groups.

TIMING
20 minutes.

HOME LINKS
Invite parents and carers to come in and cook with groups of children.

FOLLOW-UP IDEAS
Try other foods from the Caribbean.

• • • • • •

Follow recipes that reflect the foods eaten by other groups who have come to this country such as roti, pizzas and fortune cookies.

• • • • • •

Make or taste foods linked with festivals such as coconut barfi for Eid and Divali.

BANANA CAKE

Learning objective
To find out about recipes that reflect the culture and traditions of people living in Britain today.

What you need
450g self-raising flour; 175g butter; 225g brown sugar; four ripe bananas; two eggs; 1 teaspoon baking powder; greased loaf tin; mixing bowls; mixer; sieve (optional); spoon; fork and scales.

Preparation
Set the oven to 180°C (350°F) Gas Mark 4. Measure out the ingredients. **NB** Check for any allergies and dietary requirements.

What to do
Ask the children to wash their hands thoroughly and explain why it is important to do so. Let the children take it in turns to do different parts of the mixing and making. Break the bananas into a bowl and mash them well. Cream the butter and sugar together. Add the bananas to the mixture and mix with a spoon. Sieve the flour and baking powder before folding this into the bowl. When well mixed, put the mixture into the loaf tin. Bake for approximately 45 minutes.

When firm to the touch, it should be removed from the oven by an adult. When cold, cut and share among the group.

While the cake is cooking, talk to the children about the ingredients. Discuss what they think will happen to them when they are cooked. Talk about where bananas come from. What ideas do the children have about how and where bananas grow? Tell the children that lots of the bananas we eat come from the Caribbean. Explain that bananas are often grown on large farms or plantations that employ many people. Bananas are picked when green and carefully wrapped and boxed. Talk about the Caribbean and explain that many people from there have come to live in England.

Support
Help the children when the mixture becomes hard to stir.

Extension
Discuss the Caribbean in greater detail with the children. Explain to them that it is an area made up of lots of different islands. The Caribbean is warmer than England, so different foods such as sugar, oranges, mango and maize are able to grow there.

SOUNDS

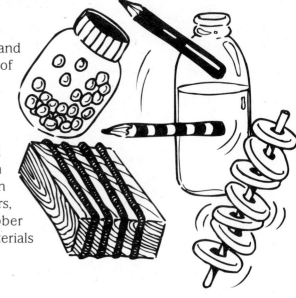

Learning objective
To listen to the sounds and explore the materials of different instruments.

What you need
Cassette player; example of steel band music (available from most libraries); selection of boxes, fabrics, papers, sticks, string and rubber bands; glue; dried materials (for shaking).

Preparation
Listen to the music and set out the materials.

What to do
Listen to the music together and talk about how it makes the children feel. Do they want to sit still or move to the beat? What instruments do they think are being used? Explain a little about how people that were captured as slaves made music by using the materials that they could find, including steel drums. What could the children use? Use objects in the room to bang, pluck or shake.

Give small groups of children a selection of materials so that they can experiment with making their own instruments. Ideas include placing long rubber bands around an open box to pluck, or pouring water in a milk bottle and hitting it gently with a pencil. Encourage them to vary the size, material, tension and shape. Does it make a difference if they use their fingers or an implement to bang or pluck? Does the size and amount of material make any difference when shaking? Talk about the variations and the effects of the changes.

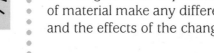

Support
Limit the materials available and provide guidance when assembling the instruments. Help the children to select appropriate materials.

Extension
Encourage the children to make predictions about their instruments and to think of ways to vary the sound. Provide a wide selection of materials such as different materials for a drum so that the children can predict if the sounds will be louder or quieter.

GROUP SIZE
Whole group.

TIMING
Ten minutes.

MAKING JOURNEYS

Learning objectives
To examine reasons why people make journeys.

What you need
Two bags or suitcases – one packed with clothes and toiletries for the weekend; the other for a long break in a hot country; a bag of shopping such as a supermarket carrier bag with some shopping items.

Preparation
Prepare the cases in such a way that the children cannot see the contents.

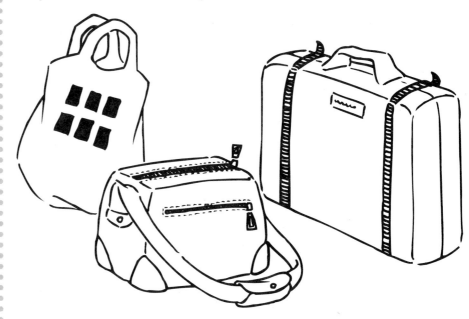

What to do
Show the children the shopping bag and its contents. Ask them to imagine who it belongs to. Ask them who has been on a journey. Where did they go? How did they get there? How long did they stay? What did they do there? How were they welcomed? Repeat the process with the weekend bag. Ask similar questions but encourage a wider variety of answers. Combine the children's answers to develop into a short story about the reason for the journey.

Now show the children the suitcase and ask them to think of some of the reasons for a long journey. Is it to visit relatives? Did someone in the family live there previously? What feelings are associated with such a long journey? How will the person get there? Will they be coming back to stay? Encourage the children to think about refugees who might only arrive with one suitcase or bag.

Support
Ask the children to say what things they might need to bring for their journey to the group such as a packed lunch, coat and sweater.

Extension
Add items to the luggage that would indicate going on a pilgrimage such as the Muslim Hajj. (Try the local Education Centre for items such as a prayer mat.) Talk about pilgrimages with older children.

HOME LINKS

Ask parents and carers to discuss journeys with their child. Can their child remember a visit or journey that they made? Encourage them to let their child help to pack (or at least think of what is needed) when they next go on holiday or to visit a friend or relative.

FOLLOW-UP IDEAS

Make a display all about journeys including tickets, receipts, luggage labels, brochures and so on.

••••••

Plan to go on a bus journey with the children. Discuss with them suitable clothing, cost, route and so on.

GROUP SIZE
Small groups.

TIMING
Five to ten minutes
a day.

HOME LINKS
Ask parents and
carers to encourage
their child to use
descriptive language
and all their senses
as well as sight.

**FOLLOW-UP
IDEAS**
Use the senses
across all the
activities of the day.
For example, talk
about smells and
textures when
cooking; colours
when painting or
the feel of wet and
dry sand.

· · · · · ·

Make an interactive
display using
materials from the
main activity. Label
with the descriptive
words that the
children used. Help
individual children
to use a word-
processing package
to produce the
labels.

· · · · · ·

Demonstrate how
materials can
change, such as
spices when cooked
and dry paint mixed
with water.

THE SENSES

Learning objective
To use the senses to examine products that reflect multicultural Britain.

What you need
Provide spoons and a selection of items to stimulate each of the senses, such as: *smell* – pepper, ripe guava, spices; *hearing* – music, a brown coconut containing liquid (you can hear it when shaken); *taste* – pizza, noodles, lime; *touch* – sari fabric, statue of Ganesha, rosary beads, coconut; *sight* – examples of writing in different languages, pictures of artefacts such as the Star of David, Lion of Judah and a paper dragon.

What to do
Prepare a selection of items for each of the five senses that depict multicultural Britain. Mix these with items that are familiar to the children. It might help if the children close their eyes or wear a blindfold initially. They can then guess what the item is.

Talk about the items and ask the children to discuss their preferences. Point out that someone else might have a different reaction. Ask them to describe the item and what they think about it. Encourage them to use vocabulary such as sweet, bitter, tingly, loud, crumbly and bumpy.

Support
Young children are often unsure about tasting new foods. Encourage them but do not pressurize them. Start with more familiar items before trying the new ones. Some children may not be happy about wearing a blindfold, so let them just close their eyes.

Extension
Choose one object for the children to examine in detail using as many of the senses as possible. Ask them to describe it in their own words.

GROUP SIZE
Whole group.

GROUP SIZE
Whole group.

TIMING
Five minutes.

HOME LINKS
Make a display of the kind of animal life that might be found in and around the home such as butterflies, woodlice, worms, birds and frogs. Ask parents and carers to encourage their child to look for the animals and to observe them without disturbing them. Back at the group, talk to the children about what they have seen.

FOLLOW-UP IDEAS

Set up a bird-table and feed the birds appropriately for the time of year.

• • • • • •

Plant a buddleia or other butterfly-loving plant.

• • • • • •

Make a big book of pets and ways to care for them. Use the children's own words whenever possible.

ANIMAL CARE

Learning objective
To link the care of animals with the festival of Wesak.

What you need
Writing materials; paper; pictures of pets and farm animals.

What to do
Explain to the children that Wesak is a festival that is very important to Buddhists. Buddhists are people who follow the teachings of the Buddha. The Buddha travelled around teaching people that they should be unselfish, kind to each other and caring to all living things. He considered that animals were his friends and should be treated as such.

Now talk to the children about ways to be kind to animals. Together, draw up a list of things that pets need such as food, water, care and so on. What animals do the children see in their daily lives and on television? Make a list of all the pets that the children have. This could also take the form of a graph. Extend their thoughts to wild animals, insects, frogs and other creatures that might be found in gardens or the local area. How can they be kind to them? If you have a group pet such as a gerbil or a hamster, encourage the children to share in its care.

Support
Show the children pictures of pets and farm animals to help them learn and remember their names. Talk about ways to look after pets. What can the children do?

Extension
Concentrate on garden wildlife and wild animals which may be less familiar to the children. Discuss ways to encourage butterflies, birds and hedgehogs into their gardens or playground.

PATCHWORK MEMORIES

Learning objective
To develop an understanding of the past.

What you need
An artefact from your own past and one from a country outside Britain.

Preparation
Prepare and rehearse a story that explains your artefact, and gather some information about the artefact from another country.

What to do
Show the children an artefact that has had a connection with your own past. It could be a piece of fabric, an old photograph or an old toy. Tell them a story about its history – either real or imaginary. During the telling, include information such as the reason you had it, what you did with it, how you felt about it and what it makes you think of. Explain that you can remember people that you knew and lots of things that happened to you in the past. These are called memories. Do the children have any special memories?

   Now show the children an artefact from another country. Encourage the children to ask questions so that they can find out as much as possible about its history. If necessary, suggest questions to get them started such as, 'What is it made from? How much did it cost?'. (Answer in the currency of the country.) Throughout the question-and-answer session try to build up a picture of the country and period.

   Explain to the children that people who study things that happened in the past are called historians. Tell them that there are two main ways in which historians find out about the past – they examine objects and listen to people's memories – just like the children have done!

Support
Give the children additional prompts when asking questions. Choose an object that has a clear connection with a different country such as a model pyramid.

Extension
Record your anecdote with captions. Make it into a group book and display the artefact alongside it.

In this chapter you will find eight activities closely linked to the area of physical development. Among other things, the children will be encouraged to move to music from around the world, take part in a lion dance and develop their manipulative skills by making multicultural jewellery.

Physical development

GROUP SIZE
Whole group.

TIMING
Five minutes.

HOME LINKS
Encourage parents and carers to let their child listen to a variety of music at home.

FOLLOW-UP IDEAS
Learn a dance appropriate to a particular festival such as bhangra dancing at the Sikh festival of Baisakhi.

• • • • • •

Gradually listen to longer and more varied pieces of music.

• • • • • •

Find out about the instruments used in different types of music.

MOVE TO MUSIC

Learning objective
To move or dance to music from different countries.

What you need
Space to move freely; a variety of pieces of music – South African music, the pan pipes of the Andes, salsa music and Jamaican reggae are all relatively easy to obtain – many are available from public libraries; cassette or CD player.

Preparation
Listen to the music and select a short piece. Set it up ready to play.

What to do
Ask the children to listen to the music quietly. Gradually introduce arm movements in time with the music. Stand still and sway, then move around the room to the mood of the music. Vary the type of music played to encourage a variety of movements. Ask the children to suggest different ways to move to the music such as fast and jerky, slow and floating, high and low.

Talk about the music and tell the children a little bit about the country of origin. For example, describe the mountainous area that is home of the Andean pan pipes, or the urban environment of reggae.

Support
Encourage all of the children to take part, even if it just means swaying their arms. Start with a piece that is familiar to them, such as nursery songs or soundtracks from popular children's movies, such as the Disney films.

Extension
Develop the movement into a dance that can be repeated and demonstrated to others.

GROUP SIZE
Whole group.

TIMING
Ten minutes.

HOME LINKS
Organize a
performance of the
children's favourite
movements and
invite parents and
carers to come and
watch.

**FOLLOW-UP
IDEAS**
Take photographs
of the movements
and use them to
form a display,
together with
relevant captions.
Parental consent
should be sought
before displaying
photographs of the
children.

• • • • • •

Make a group list of
the adjectives used
to describe the
movements.

• • • • • •

Talk about the
animals, transport
and weather in our
country.

MAKE THE ACTIONS

Learning objectives

To think about the animals, transport and weather in different countries and to move and depict these in an appropriate way.

What you need

Pictures of animals, transport and types of weather from information books and poster packs; an open space with room for the children to move freely.

What to do

Choose a country that is relevant to other work in the group. For example, it might be a country that you have come across when reading a story, or it might be a country that a child has recently visited. The example given (the Caribbean) can be adapted to suit the area selected.

Talk about the animals, transport and weather that are likely to be encountered in the chosen country. Ask the children to find a space and to listen as you describe the different things. Can they move appropriately as you describe each one? Examples from the Caribbean might include:

Animals

Fish – swimming with gentle and smooth curvy movements.
Mongoose – fast and darting movements.

Transport

Country bus – chugging up the hill and then going quickly down the bendy roads.

Weather

People moving slowly in the hot sunshine – fanning themselves to keep cool.
People hurrying to find shelter from the torrential, warm rain.

Add extra ideas from the children's suggestions and praise their attempts, encouraging them to be as original as possible.

Support

Demonstrate the movements for the children before encouraging them to make their own choices.

Extension

Ask groups of children to concentrate on one movement and then perform them for the other children. Try adding some percussion accompaniment.

LION DANCING

Learning objective
To perform a lion dance.

What you need
Cassette player; hoop; red and gold crêpe paper; egg boxes; red and gold ribbons; sticky tape; glue; scissors; video or appropriate music (there is a BBC *Watch* video available on the theme of Chinese New Year, but look out for other television programmes that are broadcast during January and February (the video should also contain suitable music)); a copy of 'The story of Chinese New Year' on the photocopiable sheets on pages 61 and 62.

Preparation
Familiarize yourself with the music and dance. Decorate the hoop to resemble a 'lion's head' – make features from egg boxes, hold the hoop in a vertical position and attach the features, decorate the head with red and gold materials.

What to do
Tell the children 'The story of Chinese New Year' on pages 61 and 62. Show them the video or listen to appropriate music. Explain that lion dancing is one of the ways to celebrate Chinese New Year. Traditionally, lions take part in processions and dance along the road to shops and houses. Money is hung from windows and the dancers try to catch it. It is hoped that the dancing will bring good luck during the following year.

Play the music again and ask the children to move with the music individually. Introduce the hoop and let the children take it in turns to be the leader. Line the children up behind the leader with each one holding the waist of the one in front. Replay the music and ask the group to move as a team, dancing around the room.

Support
Make individual masks of the lion's head with the children so that they can dance on their own, holding the masks to their faces. Make them by decorating a paper plate with egg box features and painting it in yellow and red (the colours associated with the festival). Attach a 'stick' of rolled-up paper.

Extension
Attach a long piece of cloth to the hoop so that it will drape over a team of children. Decorate with red and gold or yellow. Lead the lion in the dance around the room.

GROUP SIZE
Whole group divided into three groups.

TIMING
Ten minutes.

HOME LINKS
Ask parents and carers to play rowing games at home with their child such as 'Row, Row, Row Your Boat'.

FOLLOW-UP IDEAS
Make small boats with different materials and hold races in a water tray. Propel them by blowing with straws and ask the children to predict and record the results.

• • • • • •

Make models of dragon boats using recyclable materials or modelling materials such as Plasticine.

• • • • • •

The festival takes place on the fifth day of the fifth month of the lunar year. Talk to the children about the ordinal numbers – first to fifth.

DRAGON BOAT

Learning objective

To work in teams and create movements similar to those used in dragon boats.

What you need

Narrow elastic; flame-coloured tissue – sufficient to make two wristbands for each child; a copy of 'The story of the Dragon Boat Race' on the photocopiable sheet on page 64.

Preparation

Make two wristbands for each child by tying strips of flame-coloured tissue to elastic, cut and tied to size.

What to do

Read the story on page 64 to the children and explain that dragon boat races take place today and are a reminder of this story. Nowadays, the ceremonial boats hold up to 100 people but the racing boats will hold teams of 20 people. Racing is becoming more popular in Britain now.

Ask the children to sit in three columns with their legs placed on each side of the child in front. Give two wristbands to each child. Ask them to try a rowing action, bending forwards then back, and encourage them to work together. Can they suggest ways to make the rowing easier? Ask two groups to perform while the others shout encouragement. Let the children change over so that they all have a turn. Together, talk about the need to work as a team.

Support

Place an adult with each group of children to assist them with the 'racing'.

Extension

Use very large cardboard boxes to make a 'boat'. Make holes for the oars to go through. Make the 'oars' from rolled-up newspaper.

TAKING PART

Learning objective
To take part in activities based on speed, strength and skill.

What you need
Selection of skittles, hoops, balls and poles suitable for the activities selected.

Preparation
Prepare the individual activities – mark lines to stand behind when throwing; establish start and finish lines for races and set out the obstacle course. Send invitations to families to come and watch the events.

What to do
Divide the children into two groups with adults supporting each group. Give the children the opportunity to participate in each event and encourage them to compete to the best of their ability. Make sure that the mix of activities allows all of the children to experience success – not just the fastest runners. They could include:
● skittle competitions – skittles can be made by weighting pop bottles with sand
● throwing a beanbag for distance or accuracy
● running in different directions
● crawling on the ground or under a sheet
● obstacle course race – making use of materials that are readily available such as through a hoop, around a table, along a bench or marked line, under a cloth or table
● balancing a beanbag on the head or on an outstretched arm.
   Praise all of the children for taking part and for their efforts. Make sure that they feel successful in some way.
   Explain to the children that in some parts of India, Sikhs celebrate a festival called Holla Maholla in which people take part in music, poetry and sporting competitions. The festival was introduced by Guru Gobind Singh as an alternative to the Hindu festival of Holi. It was used as part of army training.

Support
Ensure that the activities are appropriate to the age and development of the children, for example, by reducing the throwing distances or enlarging targets. Provide extra adult helpers.

Extension
Increase the level of difficulty of the tasks by increasing distances to throw, using a smaller hoop and so on.

GROUP SIZE

Whole group divided into small groups.

TIMING

20 minutes.

HOME LINKS

Invite parents and carers to show any special or unusual jewellery to the children.

FOLLOW-UP IDEAS

Use the children's work to create a jewellery shop in the role-play area.

● ● ● ● ● ●

Make a display of the designs. If possible, include photographs of Indian jewellery.

● ● ● ● ● ●

Talk about other forms of body decoration such as make-up or mehndi.

BEAUTIFUL BEADS

Learning objective

To develop manipulative skills by making some Indian-style jewellery.

What you need

Illustrations of Indian jewellery found in information books; thread and blunt needle; string, wool and plastic string; cocktail sticks; spray paint (adult use only); glue; scissors; selection of craft materials such as milk-bottle tops, wool, string, pasta, corrugated card, card, play dough, small, gold cake cases and cardboard rolls; scrap materials to decorate.

What to do

Show the children the illustrations and explain that they are going to make some jewellery. Boys may be interested to know that lots of men wear jewellery and that many of the best jewellers are men. They may like to make the jewellery for their mum or a friend.

Set up the tables with different types of material and let the groups move around in rotation to try the ideas suggested below. Great care must be taken with all small items and the children must be closely supervised during the activities.

● Thread together washed milk-bottle tops.
● Roll up thin strips of corrugated card and stick down to form beads.
● Curl thin tapered strips of paper around a pencil to form beads.
● Make beads from play dough, pierce with a cocktail stick and thread onto pieces of thin, plastic string.
● Thread small, gold paper cake cases and tie a knot between each one.
● Make bangles from split cardboard rolls and decorate with scrap material 'jewels'.
● Thread commercially-produced beads.
● Stick wool or string onto small pieces of card. Make holes to form pendants.

Let an adult spray-paint the finished jewellery. Encourage the children to wear their jewels and tell them about Indian festivals and weddings.

Support

Provide extra help at all stages, from starting to roll the paper, to helping with threading and tying knots.

Extension

Give the children the opportunity to design their own jewellery based on the designs given. Encourage them to select suitable materials for the task.

GREETINGS!

Learning objective
To use a range of skills and materials to make cards for special occasions.

What you need
Pieces of A4-size card; pencils; colouring and decorative materials; scissors; glue; a copy of the photocopiable sheet 'Diva card' on page 76 per child.

Preparation
Make a demonstration card and prepare the craft materials.

What to do
Show the children the example that you made. Talk about the design and how it relates to the special occasion (such as children playing games for Holi or a diva lit during Divali). Ideas for cards for the different festivals include:
- Chinese cut-paper work (Chinese New Year)
- special menorah (Hanukkah)
- snowman or poinsettia (Christmas)
- geometric designs (Eid)
- children sprinkling coloured water on each other (Holi)
- divas (Divali).

Making a diva card
Give the children a copy of the photocopiable sheet on page 76 and ask them to decorate the diva in individual ways. Use flame-coloured materials for the flame, such as rolled-up tissue-paper balls or glitter.

Now fold the card in half and help the children to match the edges. Help the children to cut out their finished divas (providing extra assistance to cut out the difficult flame shape). Open the card and stick the edges of the diva across the middle, taking care not to stick it down flat so that it stands out from the page, giving a three-dimensional effect. Fold the card carefully so that the diva stands up when the card is opened. Write 'Happy Divali' under the diva and a greeting inside.

Support
Younger children may need the card to be prepared for them. Let them practise their cutting and sticking skills at the decorating stage of the activity.

Extension
Talk about the use of cards and the way in which they relate to the festival.

JIGGLING JIGSAWS

Learning objective

To make and complete multicultural-themed jigsaws.

What you need

Pictures from catalogues or back covers from *Nursery Projects* magazine (from issue no 17 to issue no 28, published by Scholastic Ltd, tel: 01926-813910 for back copies and subscriptions) showing children from a variety of cultural and religious backgrounds doing everyday activities such as shopping or playing, plus pictures of specific or cultural activities such as lighting a menorah candle or attending a Holi bonfire; A5- or A4-size card for each child; scissors; glue; examples of jigsaws with different sized and shaped cuts.

Preparation

Cut the pieces of card to fit the pictures.

HOME LINKS
Explain how the jigsaws are made so that children and parents and carers can repeat the activity together at home.

FOLLOW-UP IDEAS
Use a large picture to make a group jigsaw.

Make jigsaws as gifts for families. These could be from children's own artwork or designs made on the computer.

Have similar discussions based on illustrations in books, cards and so on.

What to do

Show the children the choice of pictures and baseboards and ask them to choose one. Discuss the pictures together. Are there any features that they find unusual or new? Talk about the differences as well as the similarities such as a Christian child might go to Sunday school and a Muslim child might go to the Mosque, but they both enjoy playing and shopping with their mums. Be willing to talk about skin and hair colouring in a positive way.

Now show the children how to stick the picture on the card and help them to smooth it down. While the glue is drying, show the children pieces from real jigsaws. Talk about the shapes of the pieces. Do they want to make straight or curved cuts? How many pieces do they want?

When completely dry, ask the children to draw the jigsaw lines on the back prior to cutting. Cut the picture into the desired number of pieces and challenge the children to piece them together again. Encourage them to try each other's jigsaws.

Support

The children will need help with the cutting and sticking. Limit the number of pieces to just three for younger children.

Extension

Make double-sided jigsaws by sticking a second picture on the back of the card. See if the children can reconnect the pictures correctly.

Multicultural activities lend themselves readily to this area of learning and the eight activities in this chapter make good use of different cultural patterns and art. The children will also have opportunities to listen and respond to a range of different types of music and make decorations for some popular festivals.

Creative development

GROUP SIZE
Small groups.

TIMING
20 minutes.

HOME LINKS
Ask parents and carers to talk to the children about the ways in which they prepare for celebrations. They can also discuss ways in which dyes and make-up are used.

FOLLOW-UP IDEAS
Use the hands to decorate cards for Eid, Holi or Divali.

• • • • • •

Find out about other hand and body decorations.

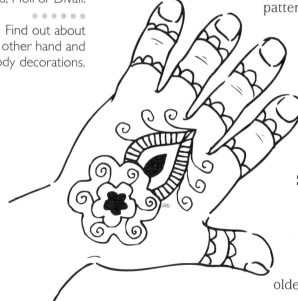

MEHNDI

Learning objective
To produce patterns for hand decoration.

What you need
'The story of the mehndi tree' on the photocopiable sheet on page 65; the photocopiable sheet 'Mehndi characters' on page 77; paper (preferably skin toned); colouring materials; pencils; scissors; the photocopiable sheet 'Mehndi patterns' on page 78.

Preparation
Cut out and colour the characters from the photocopiable sheet on page 77.

What to do
Tell the children 'The story of the mehndi tree' on page 65, using the cut-out characters from page 77. Explain that women and girls throughout the Indian subcontinent and Indian women in Britain wear this kind of decoration, especially for weddings and other religious celebrations. The designs can be very complicated and often contain the shape of the popular fruit, the mango – the shape that features in the paisley pattern. Designs stain the skin and can last for several weeks.

Explain that you would like the children to create their own designs on paper. Show them the examples on the photocopiable sheet 'Mehndi patterns' on page 78. Ask the children to draw around their hands and then to decorate the hand shapes with mehndi patterns, referring to the examples on the photocopiable sheet. Cut out the completed hands and display them.

Support
Draw around the children's hands for them and then cut out the completed hands for them.

Extension
Use the more complicated examples of decoration with older children.

LISTEN AND RESPOND

Learning objective
To respond to music from a variety of cultures.

What you need
Music from different cultures such as bhangra from India, Greek traditional dance music, Christmas calypso music (often available from local libraries); cassette or CD player.

Preparation
Listen to the music and select the part to be used.

What to do
Ask the children to sit still and comfortably. Try to make sure that there are no distractions. Suggest that the children close their eyes to help them to concentrate. Play a short piece of the music and listen to it together.

Talk to the children about how you feel when you listen to the music. Ask them how it makes them feel. Did they want to get up and dance, drift into sleep or clap to the beat? Were there any other responses? Help the children to understand that music can help to create atmosphere. For example, does the Christmas calypso music make the children think of snowmen and robins or of celebrating in a warm climate? Some children might not respond to the music or have the language to express their feelings. Replay the piece and remind the children of some of the responses. Repeat the activity later with different music.

Support
Only expect the children to concentrate for short periods of time. Encourage them to act out their feelings if the vocabulary is difficult.

Extension
Talk about the music in more detail. Discuss the country of origin and the type of instruments used. Ask the children to imagine how Christmas is celebrated in warm climates.

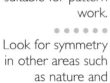

ISLAMIC PATTERNS

Learning objective
To create patterns based on the geometric patterns
found in Islamic art.

What you need
Coloured card; paper (slightly smaller than the card);
glue; materials for decorating such as small gummed
shapes; crayons; felt-tipped pens; examples of
Islamic patterns from art and festivals books from
local libraries (optional).

Preparation
Make a symmetrical pattern from the shapes and
add a border of geometric shapes or writing patterns
to show to the children. Prepare the area for a craft
activity.

What to do
Show the children some examples of Islamic patterns
(if available) and show them the one that you have
made. Explain that these special kinds of patterns
are symmetrical – that both sides of the pattern are
the same. Help them to see the symmetry with both
sides matching. The geometric shapes in the Islamic
patterns are always used in an art form that never
depicts humans or animals.

Suggest that the children try to make one of these
patterns using sticky shapes. Ask the children to fold
the smaller sheet in half and then open it to form a
crease. Stick a shape on one side and then find an
exact copy to place on the other side. Repeat with
other shapes. Encourage the children to make the
patterns as symmetrical as possible.

When complete, stick the paper in the centre of a
larger contrasting sheet of card. Show the children
how to make a border using geometric shapes and
writing patterns.

Support
Simplify the patterns and shapes used. Use the words
'same' and 'different' and encourage observation of
size, shape and colour.

Extension
Fold the smaller pieces of paper into four and match
the four pieces.

GROUP SIZE
Small groups.

TIMING
15 minutes.

HOME LINKS
Ask the children to make a detailed drawing of one of their favourite toys at home. Suggest that they bring it to your group to show to their friends.

FOLLOW-UP IDEAS
Prepare a display with questions such as, 'Which fruit has a furry skin? Which fruit has sharp leaves?'.

• • • • • •

Create an additional display for the drawings that the children did at home. Ask the children for suitable captions.

• • • • • •

Encourage the children to look closely at other things, such as the flowers on the way to the group.

• • • • • •

Look at the still-life paintings of well-known artists.

LOOKING CLOSELY

Learning objective
To learn to look closely at objects.

What you need
Selection of fruits such as star fruit, lychee, pineapple or ripe mango; paper; pencils or crayons.

Preparation
Prepare the area for drawing, arrange the seating so that all the children can see the object clearly.

What to do
Choose a fruit such as a lychee to show to the children – try to make it something that is unfamiliar to all of them. Ask them to look at it really carefully. Can they describe the shape, colour and texture? Talk about shady or light parts. Describe the shading on the skin of the lychee. Does the fruit have a stalk or root?

Encourage the description of detail although this might not be produced in the drawing. Ask the children to draw the item on their table – remembering the points discussed. As they work, talk about the object itself. Where does it come from? Is it a hot or cold country? How is it used? How did it come to this country?

Support
Choose an object that has a fairly simple shape such as a mango. Paint or large crayons might be more suitable than pencils for the children to use.

Extension
Ask the children to provide more detail in their drawings. Encourage them to match the exact colour, shape and size.

GROUP SIZE
Small group.

TIMING
20 minutes.

HOME LINKS
Invite parents and carers to a performance of the story, with the children using the puppets that they have made. Suggest that parents and carers tell their children the traditional story of Pinocchio the puppet.

FOLLOW-UP IDEAS
Make other forms of puppets such as sock or glove puppets.

Provide puppets to encourage quiet children to participate in stories and to extend their use of language.

PUPPET FUN

Learning objective
To make a puppet after examining a range of different styles.

What you need
Examples of a range of puppets or pictures of them; 'The story of Divali' on the photocopiable sheet on pages 58 and 59 or 'The story of Chinese New Year' on the photocopiable sheets on pages 61 and 62; drawing or painting materials; paper plates; card; scissors; canes/sticks/rolled paper; glue; sticky tape.

What to do
Look closely at the pictures or puppets and talk about the way that they have been made. What materials are they made of? How have the parts been fixed together? Have the puppets been made to go with any particular story? Explain that some special stories such as the Hindu Divali story are told all over the world using elaborate shadow puppets. The Chinese New Year story about the animals' race is often told using shadow puppets.

Explain that the children are going to design and make their own stick puppet that can also be used as a shadow puppet with the addition of light and a screen or white wall.

Choose either 'The story of Divali' on pages 58 and 59 or 'The story of Chinese New Year' on pages 61 and 62 and read it to the children. Talk about the characters and the way that they might have looked. Ask the children to draw or paint large pictures of the characters in the story on paper plates and help them to attach sticks or rolled-up newspaper. Encourage the children to add extra features such as ears on the hare. Retell the story and ask the children to join in with their puppets at the appropriate times.

Support
Choose a more familiar story or a nursery rhyme for the children's first attempt at puppet play.

Extension
Make more elaborate puppets by adding joints to the figures using card and paper fasteners.

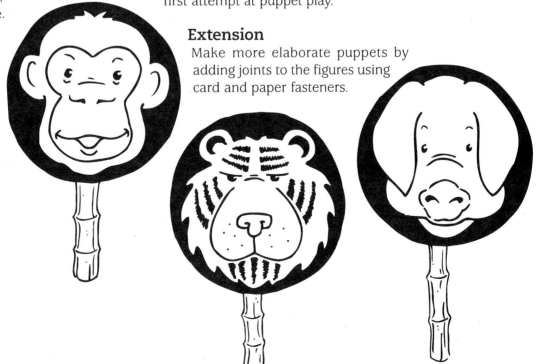

GROUP SIZE
Small groups.

TIMING
20 minutes.

HOME LINKS
Ask parents and carers to observe the phases of the moon and talk about the changes with their child. Encourage them to record their observations on a simple sheet. Provide them with copies of the photocopiable sheet on page 79, showing the phases of the moon.

FOLLOW-UP IDEAS
Celebrate the festival of Eid by making cards and appropriate food, such as Indian sweets.

Experiment with changing the length of the string or the size of the shapes. Which shapes and sizes do the children like best?

Talk about waiting for the new moon. How do the children feel when they have to wait for a special occasion?

MOVING MOBILES

Learning objective

To make mobiles for festivals such as Eid.

What you need

Card; string; foil; glitter; glue; scissors; sharp pencil for making holes (adult use only); the photocopiable sheet 'Moon observations' on page 79.

Preparation

Make a large star from card and foil and attach some string for hanging. Cut out star and moon shapes from card for the children. Make holes in them to thread string.

What to do

Tell the children about the Islamic festival of Eid.

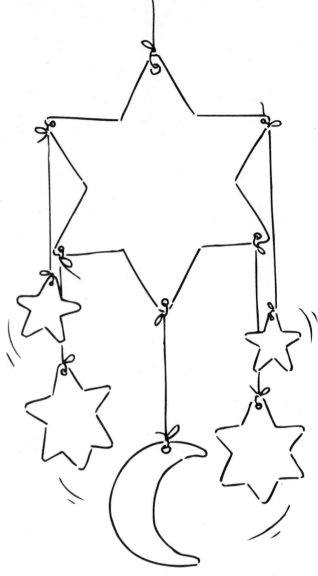

Explain that the celebration of Eid takes place when the adults in the family have been fasting from dawn to dusk for a month. When the new moon arrives, they start their festivities.

Tell the children that they are going to make some decorations to celebrate the festival of Eid. Give them a choice of a star or a moon and explain that they are the special symbols of Islam, so they are appropriate as decorations for Eid. Ask the children to cover one side of the shape with foil. Stick it in place with small amounts of glue, smooth it down and trim it to make it neat. Place spots of glue on the other side of the shape and sprinkle with glitter. Shake off the excess and allow to dry. Tie string to each piece and attach to the large star that you made earlier. Adjust the lengths to balance the mobile. Hang in a position where it can flow freely.

Support

Provide the children with extra help with the cutting and tying as necessary.

Extension

Let the children make their own drawings of stars and moons. Talk about the shape of the moon and how it changes.

GROUP SIZE
Small groups.

TIMING
20 minutes.

HOME LINKS
Invite parents and carers to a performance of the story. Use torn-up pieces of tissue to throw over the audience.

FOLLOW-UP IDEAS
Talk about the story and the way in which Prahlada resisted temptation. How can the children try to do the right thing? Are there times when they feel tempted, such as if they find an object that they would like to keep for themselves rather than return it, or joining in when someone is calling somebody names?

Think of some tricks that the children would like to play on adults. These must be safe and kind, but with an element of fun.

Celebrate the festival with decorations and food such as mild samosas and Indian sweets.

FLICK AND SPLATTER!

Learning objective
To create splatter paintings for decoration at the Hindu festival of Holi.

What you need
'The story of Holi' on the photocopiable sheet on page 57; brightly-coloured paint; large sheets of paper; old brushes such as toothbrushes; aprons; paper to cover tables.

Preparation
Ask the children to put aprons on and cover the area to be used with paper to protect it.

What to do
Tell the children 'The story of Holi' on page 57. Explain that one way of celebrating the festival of Holi is for children to play practical jokes on adults, and another is for people to dress in old clothes and throw coloured water on each other. These are reminders of the playful antics of the young Lord Krishna.

Ask the children to paint large pictures of themselves. When dry, place these in the prepared area for splattering. Use old brushes to flick paint over the portraits. Help the children to select colours and to splatter the paint fairly evenly over the painting. Allow to dry before mounting or sending home (with an explanation of the splattered paint!).

Support
If the children find the flicking action difficult, add spots of glue to the portraits and let them sprinkle glitter over the paintings instead.

Extension
Examine the story in more detail and talk to the children about India and the people in the story including their appearance and clothes. Be willing to discuss skin and hair colouring.

GROUP SIZE
Large or small
groups.

TIMING
15 minutes.

HOME LINKS
Hold an exhibition
of all the children's
designs and invite
parents and carers
to view.

**FOLLOW-UP
IDEAS**
Make similar designs,
but decorate with
coloured sand or
pasta.

· · · · · ·

Make a large group
rangoli pattern and
place it at the
entrance to the
room.

· · · · · ·

Talk about other
ways to make
entrances
welcoming, such as
with balloons for a
party or a wreath at
Christmas.

RANGOLI PATTERNS

Learning objective
To make patterns for Hindu festival decorations.

What you need
The photocopiable sheet 'Rangoli patterns' on page 80 that has examples of completed rangoli designs; small pieces of tissue paper; glue.

Preparation
Copy the photocopiable sheet to A3 size several times and cut out a selection of the individual patterns ready for the children to use.

What to do
Explain that rangoli patterns were originally seen as a token of thanksgiving to the earth, which gives life to everyone. Rangoli patterns are now widely used as a form of folk art.

Tell the children that rangoli patterns are frequently seen at the entrance to a Hindu home at the time of a festival or celebration. Indeed, during the festival of Divali, competitions may take place and people are invited to view the designs. The patterns are often thought of as a welcome to a home or shop.

Show the children the designs that you have prepared and demonstrate how to stick on the pieces of tissue paper. Ask the children to start with the centre of the design and work outwards, spreading small amounts of glue and adding small, tissue-paper balls placed close to each other.

Support
Use crayons or felt-tipped pens to colour the designs rather than using the tissue paper and glue.

Extension
Ask the children to try to create their own designs on dotted paper. Start with a shape in the centre and work outwards, keeping the pattern symmetrical.

The story of Holi

Once there lived a king who thought he was God. He had a little boy called Prahlada. He told Prahlada that he was God, and Prahlada thought that this was true. When Prahlada grew up, he still thought that his father was God. One day he went for a walk. He saw a man who made pots. The man was very upset. Some kittens had climbed into a pot and gone to sleep. The potter didn't know they were there, so he put his pots into the hot oven to bake hard. He thought the kittens would die in the oven, and he was praying to God to save them. Prahlada asked, 'Are you praying to the king?'. The potter said, 'No! I'm praying to Lord Vishnu.'* Just then, they heard a little sound – 'Miaow, miaow!'. The kittens were alive! God had saved them.

Now Prahlada knew that Vishnu was God. His father was just a man! The king was so angry that he tried to kill Prahlada. His soldiers dug a pit, and filled it with snakes. They threw Prahlada into the pit, but the snakes didn't bite him, because God was looking after him. One day, when Prahlada was asleep on the grass, the king sent his elephant to walk on Prahlada and kill him. The elephant stepped carefully around Prahlada, because God was looking after him. The king sent his soldiers to kill Prahlada with sharp swords. They couldn't hurt Prahlada, because God was looking after him. The king was furious. He asked his sister Holika to help him kill Prahlada. Holika had a magic gift. Fire couldn't burn her. The king's men built a huge bonfire, and Holika said to Prahlada, 'Climb up to the top of the bonfire with me – you can see for miles.' Prahlada climbed up with Holika. When they were at the top, the soldiers lit the bonfire, and the flames leapt up round them. But God was looking after Prahlada. The fire didn't burn him. Instead, God broke Holika's magic, so that she was the one who was burnt up in the fire.

Now at Holi, people build bonfires to remind them about this story.

*Vishnu is a name that Hindu people give to God.

© Barbara Moore

The story of Divali

Once there was an old king. He had a son called Rama. Rama wanted to marry a beautiful princess called Sita. Her father had a huge bow. It was so heavy that no one could bend it. He said to Sita, 'If Rama is strong enough to bend this bow, then he is the man for you.' Rama picked up the bow. He bent it so hard that it broke into bits! Sita was very happy. She married Rama, and they went back to Rama's home.

One day, the old king sent for his sons. He said, 'I am old. One day soon, I will die. I want Rama to be the new king after me.' The queen heard about this. She was angry. She wanted her son, Bharat, to be the new king. She went to the old king and said, 'You promised to give me anything I wanted.' The king said, 'What do you want?'

'I want Bharat to be the king after you, and I want you to send Rama away.' The king was very sad, but he had to keep his promise. He sent Rama away for fourteen years. Sita went with him, and Rama's brother Lakshman went, too.

Not long after that, the old king died. The queen went to Bharat, and said, 'Now you are the new king.' But Bharat said, 'Rama should be the new king. I am going to find him.' When Bharat found Rama, he said, 'Our father is dead. Please come home and be the new king.' Rama said, 'I promised that I wouldn't come back for fourteen years.' Bharat said, 'Then give me your golden slippers. I'll put them on the king's throne to show that you are the king. I won't sit on the throne, but I will look after everything until you come back.'

Rama and Sita and Lakshman lived happily in the forest. But a wicked demon called Ravana saw Sita. He wanted her for his wife. He sent a beautiful golden deer. When Sita saw it, she cried, 'Please catch it, Rama!' Rama ran into the forest after the deer. Lakshman heard a voice calling, 'Help! Help me, Lakshman!' He thought Rama was in danger, but it was a trick. 'I must go and help Rama,' he cried. Quickly, he drew a

magic circle around Sita. 'Stay here and you will be safe,' he said, then he ran off to find Rama.

Now Sita was all by herself. The wicked demon changed himself into the shape of an old man. He pretended he was ill, so Sita came out of the magic circle to help him. At once, Ravana changed back into his own shape – a terrible demon with ten arms and ten heads. He flew away across the sea with Sita, and locked her up in his castle on the island of Lanka. Rama and Lakshman came back from the forest. They looked everywhere for Sita, but they couldn't find her.

One day, they met Hanuman, the king of the monkeys. Hanuman said, 'Ravana has got Sita. I will help you to save her, and my monkeys will help, too.' The monkeys built a bridge across the sea, and there was a fierce battle that went on for ten days. Rama prayed to God to help him, and God gave him a magic arrow. Next day, he shot the arrow straight through Ravana's heart. The wicked demon fell down dead. Rama had won!

At last the fourteen years had gone by. It was time for Rama and Sita to go home. Everyone came out with little candles* to welcome them back. Now Rama and Sita were the king and queen, and everyone was happy.

*The little candles were called divas, so that is how Divali got its name.

© Barbara Moore

The story of the banyan tree

Near a village, grew a banyan tree. Its trunk was massive, and its thick branches hung down to the ground. No one knew how old it was. When the oldest man in the village was just a little boy, the banyan tree was already very old. Everyone loved the banyan tree. People used to come and rest under it after their work in the fields. They remembered that when Buddha was a young man, he used to sit under a banyan tree and pray to god. They often said a prayer as they rested out of the hot sun.

Monkeys played in the branches at the top of the tree. An owl lived in the hollow tree trunk. Brightly-coloured birds sang among the leaves. A nest of bees lived inside the tree. Blue and green shiny beetles lived in the bark of the tree. Down among its roots lived a family of mice.

One day, a woodcutter from a different village came along. No one saw him, because everyone was working in the fields. He saw the banyan tree, and thought, 'What a splendid old tree! If I cut it down, I can sell the wood, and I shall be rich. I'll build a big house, instead of my little hut.' He took his axe from his belt to chop the tree down. All the animals and birds who lived in the tree came hurrying out to try to stop him. 'This is our home! We live here,' they all cried. 'Please don't chop it down.' But the woodcutter didn't care. 'Find somewhere else to live,' he said.

The animals and birds were very angry. The monkeys jumped on his back and pulled his hair. The birds flew round his head, and pecked his arms and face. The beetles bit his toes. The mice ran up his legs and bit them. Hundreds of bees came swarming out and stung him. 'Ow, ow, ow,' shouted the woodcutter. He dropped his axe, and ran away as fast as he could, with the swarm of bees chasing him.

The banyan tree was safe. The animals and birds came back to live in it, and the people of the village came back from work and sat under its branches.

© Barbara Moore

The story of Chinese New Year

It was nearly New Year. Twelve animals were arguing. There was a rat, an ox, a tiger, a hare, a dragon, a snake, a horse, a sheep, a monkey, a cockerel, a dog and a pig. Each one of the animals wanted the New Year to be named after himself. The rat squeaked, the ox lowed, the tiger growled, the hare squealed, the dragon roared, the snake hissed, the horse neighed, the sheep bleated, the monkey chattered, the cockerel crowed, the dog barked and the pig grunted. What a noise!

The gods heard them quarrelling, and came to see what the fuss was about. When the animals saw them, everything went quiet. 'What are you arguing about?' asked the gods. All the animals tried to tell them at once. 'One at a time!' they cried. When it was quiet, one of the gods said, 'You, Dragon. Please tell us what all this is about.' Dragon started to tell them. 'It's nearly New Year. We all want the New Year to have a name. I think the New Year should be called 'The Year of the Dragon.' All the other animals started shouting again, 'No! The New Year should be named after me!'

The gods could see that there would soon be a fight. They commanded, 'Stop this at once!' When it was quiet again, one said, 'Listen! We've thought of a way to decide who the New Year should be named after. Can you see the river over there? Well, you must have a

race to see who can swim to the other side first. We will name the New Year after the winner of the race.'

'What a good idea!' the animals all said. Each one thought that he would be the winner.

They lined up on the bank of the river. 'Ready, steady, go!' cried one of the gods. There was a mighty SPLASH! as they jumped into the water. They all swam as fast as they could. Soon Ox, who was big and strong, was in front. Little Rat was a good swimmer too. He was not far behind Ox. Rat could see Ox's tail in the water just in front of him. He grabbed hold of it, and climbed onto Ox's back. Ox thought Rat's little feet were just the water tickling him. He was nearly at the other side of the river. Just as he was going to climb out of the water, Rat jumped over his head onto the river bank. 'Hooray! I'm the winner!' shouted Rat. Ox was puzzled. 'Where did you come from?' he asked as he climbed up the bank. Rat didn't say anything – he just laughed. The gods laughed, too. 'Little Rat is the winner,' they said. 'He was too clever for you this time,

Ox. This New Year will be called The Year of the Rat. Ox, you came second, so next year will be The Year of the Ox.'

One by one, the animals finished the race. Tiger was third, Hare was fourth, Dragon was fifth, Snake was sixth, Horse was seventh, Sheep was eighth, Monkey was ninth, Cockerel was tenth, Dog was eleventh, and Pig, who was rather fat and slow, came last. The gods said, 'Well done, all of you. Each one of you deserves to have a year named after you.' And so each New Year was given the name of one of the twelve animals, in the same order that they finished the race. They were all very happy, because they all had a year named after them. Rat was happiest of all, because the very first New Year was named after him.

© Barbara Moore

The story of Hanukkah

Once there was a man called Mattathias. He lived in the city of Jerusalem, and he was a Jew. The king was not a Jew. He was Syrian, but he was a good king, and the Jews were free to pray to God in their own way. When the old king died, Antiochus became the new king. He thought the Jews should do as he told them, and pray to his gods. When the Jews wouldn't do this, the king was very angry. He sent his soldiers to Jerusalem. They killed hundreds of Jews. They stormed into the temple, where the Jews prayed to god, and stole its treasures. They used the temple for games and eating and drinking. They took the special light from the altar. This was a candlestick with seven branches, called a menorah.

The Jews couldn't use their temple any more. They were very angry and upset. Mattathias said to his sons and friends, 'We must fight back. We are not soldiers, but God is on our side. One day, we will win and get Jerusalem back.' They went to live in caves near the city. They kept attacking the Syrian soldiers when they weren't expecting it, and then hurried back to hide in the caves. Mattathias was old and he died. His son Judah became the leader. Judah told his men, 'We will not rest until Jerusalem is ours and the menorah is burning on the altar again.'

The fighting went on for two years. The people of Jerusalem had used up nearly all their food and water and oil for the lamps. It was a long, hard time. The Syrian soldiers were tired of fighting. At last, Judah and his men stormed into Jerusalem and drove them out. The Jews were free again! People came out to dance and sing in the streets because they were so happy. Then they set about cleaning the temple so that they could give thanks to God. They put the menorah on the altar. There was hardly any oil in it – just enough for one day. They prayed to God that it would keep on burning until they could get some more oil. God heard their prayers, and the menorah kept on burning for eight days.

Now Jewish people all over the world still remember this story with a festival of lights called Hanukkah.

© Barbara Moore

The story of the Dragon Boat Race

Long ago in China, there lived a wise man called Ch'u Yuan. He helped the king to decide what to do if he was not sure. He always tried to do what was best for the king and his country, because he loved them.

There was a country nearby called Chuan. Its soldiers kept attacking and robbing people in all the countries that were its neighbours. Ch'u Yuan knew about this and thought hard about what to do. At last, he went to the king and said, 'We must do something to stop the soldiers from attacking our people. They keep on stealing their food and their animals, so that the people are poor and hungry. Sometimes, if they try to fight back, they kill them.'

'What do you think we should do?' asked the king. Ch'u Yuan said, 'I think we should join up with other countries that are having the same trouble, and we should all send an army to Chuan.' The king thought about this. He didn't want a war, but he couldn't think of a way to stop the trouble. He said to Ch'u Yuan, 'I need time to think about this.' He sent Ch'u Yuan away.

Ch'u Yuan was very disappointed. Things got worse, while the king did nothing. He was so upset that he thought, 'I am going to throw myself in the river. When I am dead, the king and the people will know that I was right, then the king will do something at last.' So Ch'u Yuan went to the river and threw himself in. People who saw him were horrified. They jumped into their boats and rowed as hard as they could to try to save him, but Ch'u Yuan sank to the bottom of the deep river. No one ever found him. The people loved Ch'u Yuan, and were very sad. They wanted to stop the fish from finding his body and eating it, so they threw bamboo shoots filled with rice into the river. They thought that the fish would eat the rice instead.

Now every summer, people have Dragon Boat races to remind them of how everyone jumped into their boats to try to save Ch'u Yuan.

© Barbara Moore

The story of the mehndi tree

Once there lived a girl whose name was Rekha. Every morning, just as the dawn was lighting up the sky with red and gold, Rekha went into the garden to pick flowers. She put the flowers by the pictures and statues of gods and goddesses in the house. She always gave the prettiest flowers to Ushas, the goddess of the dawn. Rekha asked Ushas to take care of her and her family.

Rekha was a pretty girl, with long, dark, shiny hair. She was good and happy, so she had lots of friends. Sometimes she liked to sit by herself out of the hot sun in the shade of a mehndi tree. She was so quiet that the birds and the shy little deer didn't notice her there. They came to drink from the river. Rekha sat as still as a statue so that she didn't frighten them away.

Rekha grew up into a beautiful young woman, and the day came when she was going to be married. All the trees and bushes gave her flowers for her hair. The mehndi tree was sad because it had no beautiful scented flowers to give her. It remembered all the sunny days that Rekha had sat in its shade, and it said to the goddess Ushas, 'I love Rekha best of all, but I have nothing to give her on her wedding day.' The goddess smiled and said, 'Little mehndi tree, I have put the red and gold colour of the sky at dawn into your leaves. Give Rekha some of your leaves, and tell her to grind them up into a paste. Tell her to paint a pattern on her hands with the paste, and leave it on. When she washes her hands, the red and gold pattern will still be there.' The mehndi tree was delighted. It told Rekha what the goddess had said. Rekha made the mehndi paste, and carefully painted a pattern on her hands. When she washed it off, the beautiful pattern was still there. Rekha thanked the little mehndi tree, and hurried away to get ready for her wedding. Now to this day, brides still decorate their hands with mehndi patterns.

© Barbara Moore

The wise men and the elephant

It was six men of Hindustan,
To learning much inclined,
Who went to see the elephant
(Though all of them were blind),
That each by observation
Might satisfy his mind.

The first approached the elephant,
And, happening to fall
Against its broad and sturdy side,
At once began to bawl:
'Why bless me! but the elephant
Is very like a wall!'

The second, feeling at the tusk
Cried, 'Ho! what have we here
So very round and smooth and sharp?
To me it's mighty clear
This wonder of an elephant
Is very like a spear!'

The third approached the animal,
And, happening to take
The squirming trunk within his hands,
Thus boldly up he spake:
'I see', quoth he, 'the elephant
Is very like a snake!'

The fourth reached out his eager hand,
And felt about its knee
'What most this wondrous beast is like
Is mighty plain', quoth he;
'Tis clear enough the elephant
Is very like a tree!'

The fifth, who chanced to touch the ear,
Said, 'E'en the blindest man
Can tell what this resembles most;
Deny the fact who can,
This marvel of an elephant
Is very like a fan!'

The sixth no sooner had begun
About the beast to grope,
Than, seizing on the swinging tail
That fell within his scope
'I see', quoth he, 'the elephant
Is very like a rope!'

And so these wise men of Hindustan
Disputed loud and long,
Each in his own opinion
Exceeding stiff and strong;
Though each was partly in the right,
They all were in the wrong!

At least these men of Hindustan,
Who none of them had sight,
After quarrelling about the elephant,
Over different parts they did fight.
When all these parts together came,
They all of them were right!

And so we see when arguing
The best of things to do
Is listen to the other men
And see their point of view!

© John Saxe

Rhyme time

Learn this rhyme together. Make up some actions.

(Sung to the tune of 'Twinkle, Twinkle, Little Star')
Quand trois poules vont au champ,
La première va devant,
La seconde suit la première,
La troisième marche la dernière,
Quand trois poules vont au champ,
La première va devant.

When three hens go to the field,
The first one goes in front,
The second follows the first,
The third walks behind.
(Repeat the first two lines.)

Celebration parties grid

Festival	What you need	Preparation
Chinese New Year	Sweets, prawn crackers and noodles to taste; pink tissue paper; string.	Bind the twigs together with string to form a 'tree' and fix into Plasticine. Prepare the table for food.
Holi	Plain biscuits; icing; multicoloured cake decorations; large sheets of paper; aprons; old brushes (such as toothbrushes); brightly-coloured paints.	Cover the area to be used for painting. Mix the icing.
Passover	Matzot to taste; 3 large peeled potatoes; small onion; 2 eggs; 2 tablespoons flour; mixing spoon; frying pan.	Grate the potatoes and onion and mix together.
Easter	Breakfast cereal to make a bird's nest; chocolate; paper cake cases; mini Easter eggs (three or four per child); Plasticine; twigs and string to make a tree; card; scissors; decorating materials.	Join the twigs together with string to form a 'tree' and stand in a lump of Plasticine. Make templates of egg shapes if necessary and collect together decorative materials.
Eid	Indian sweets to share (available in major cities); hoop; string; green crêpe paper; scissors; glue; sticky tape; card; glitter; foil; templates of stars and crescent moons if required.	Cover the hoops with strips of green crêpe paper and make templates of stars and crescent moons if necessary.
Rastafarian New Year	115g vegetable margarine; 3 bananas; 2 tablespoons clear honey; 225g wholemeal flour; 2 teaspoons grated nutmeg; vanilla essence; 55g raisins; black pepper; red, yellow and green paint; black paper.	Prepare the ingredients as shown on page 69 and heat the oven to 180°C (350°F) Gas Mark 4.
Divali	Indian sweets to share (available from major cities); play dough.	Make the play dough if necessary.
Hanukkah	Matzot; a hanukiah; card folded to form individual greetings cards; selection of coloured and textured paper for collage; colouring materials; glue; pencils; scissors.	Find a hanukiah, or a picture of one to show to the children.

Banana cake recipe

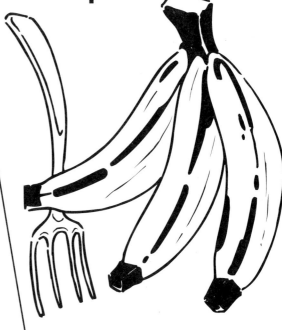

What you need
115g vegetable margarine
3 bananas
2 tablespoons clear honey
225g wholemeal flour
2 teaspoons grated nutmeg
vanilla essence
55g raisins
black pepper
20cm square cake tin
mixing bowls and spoons
a fork
a sieve

What to do
1 Heat the oven to 180°C (350°F) Gas Mark 4.
2 Cream the margarine and honey together.
3 Mash the bananas and add them to the margarine.
4 Sieve the flour and fold into the mixture.
5 Add the raisins, nutmeg and vanilla essence.
6 Pour into the cake tin and bake for 30–40 minutes.

Market stall

■ Cut out the labels and stick them next to the correct fruit and vegetables.

bananas	kiwis	sweet potatoes
peppers	coconuts	pineapple

Patterns

■ Talk about the different patterns that you can see.

Finish the shapes

■ Finish the shapes and patterns.

Complete the diva.

Complete the tree.

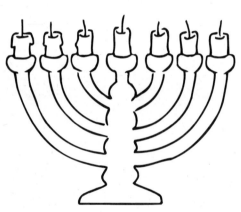

Add the flames.

Add the branches.

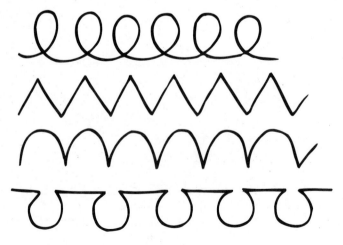

Finish the patterns.

Around the year

■ Talk about the pictures and add them to your special calendar.

Holi pictures

■ Cut out the pictures. Put them in the correct order to tell the story.

EARLY YEARS ACTIVITY CHEST Multicultural activities

A special menorah

■ Draw a new flame each day.

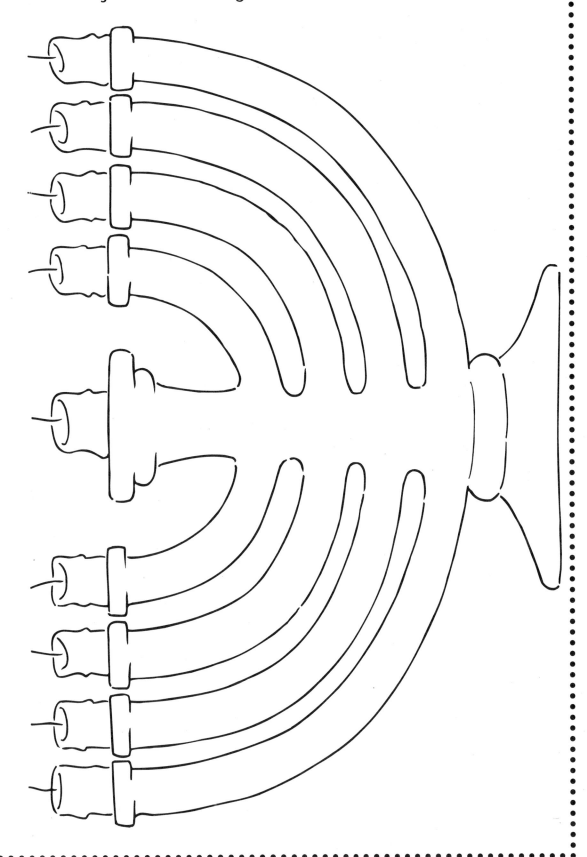

Diva card

■ Decorate the diva and cut it out.

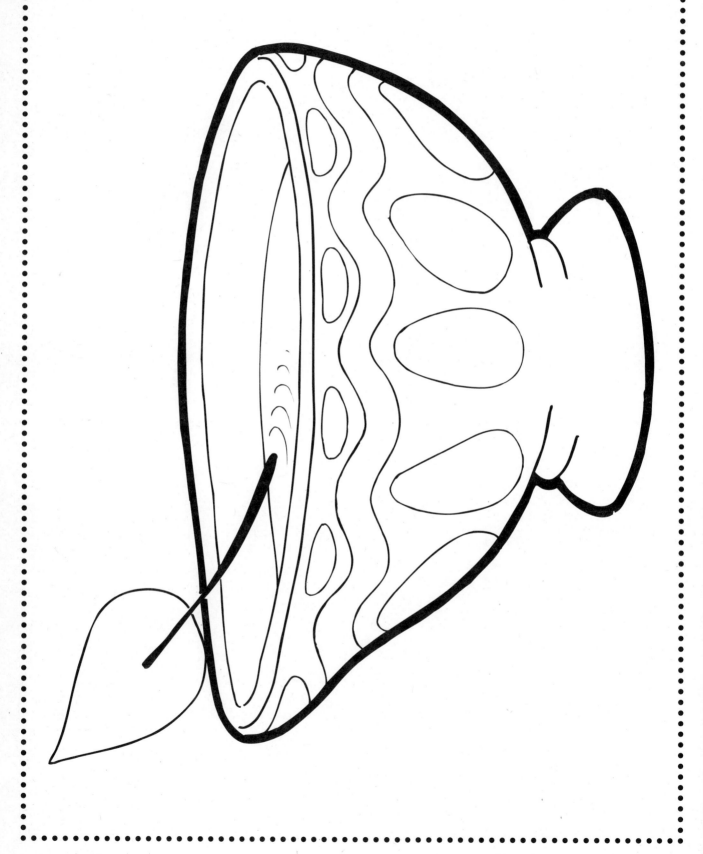

Mehndi characters

■ Cut out and decorate the characters. Use them to tell the story of the mehndi tree.

Mehndi patterns

■ Talk about the mehndi patterns. Try to make up some of your own.

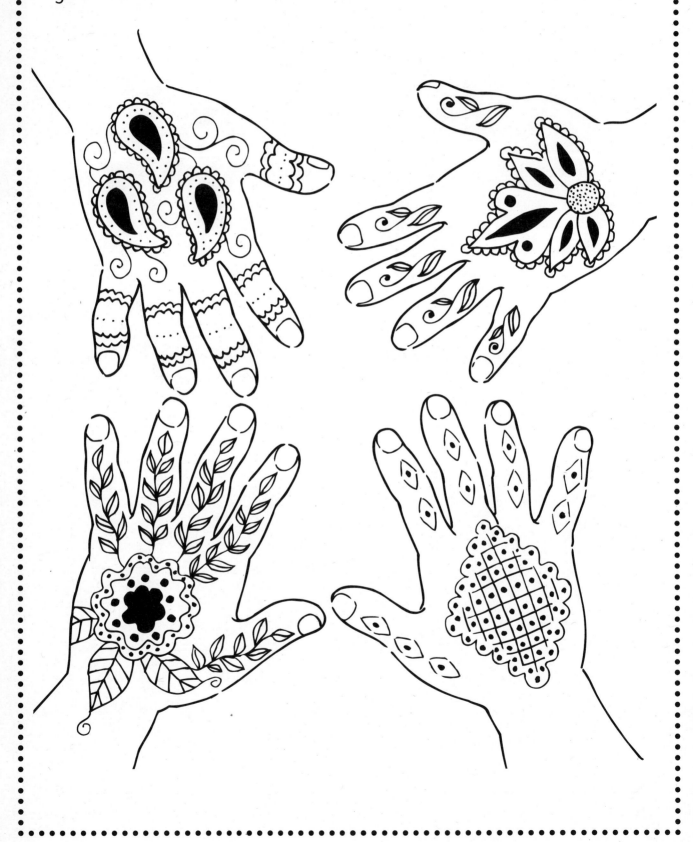

Moon observations

Sunday	Monday	Tuesday	Wednesday	Thursday	Friday	Saturday

Rangoli patterns

■ Cut out and decorate these rangoli patterns.